A New Approach to Bidding

Complete Hand Valuation (CV) and The MIDMAC Bidding System

Jon Drabble

B. T. Batsford Ltd. London

First published 1995

© Jon Drabble 1995

ISBN 0 7134 7914 0

A CIP catalogue record for this book is available from the British Library.

Typeset by Apsbridge Services Ltd, Nottingham.
Printed by Redwood Books, Trowbridge, Wiltshire
for the publishers,
B. T. Batsford Ltd, 4 Fitzhardinge Street,
London W1H 0AH

A BATSFORD BRIDGE BOOK
Series Editor: Tony Sowter

CONTENTS

PREFACE

Yes, this book will, I promise you, seem radical, controversial and maybe even anarchic. It is not for the faint-hearted, timorous or defensive, but for the courageous, open-minded bridge players who are willing to change, learn and grow. If you already recognise that bidding is the crux of bridge that will also help.

Very few players, even experts, find anything new and exciting to discover in this wonderful game of ours, although I do remember once reading a poignant foreword by Omar Sharif that talked quite emotionally about 'the undiscovered joys of bidding'. Indeed, bidding is a potential minefield of poppies, so much beauty yet to discover but it feels so dangerous if we scratch the surface too vigorously, because it might blow our minds. This book will try and take you through this field intact, but (hopefully) never the same again. I promise you an exhilarating journey, at once beautiful and exciting but at the same time a little scary.

I confess to having an obsession about bridge; it has been a life saver and saviour for me, so it is no wonder I savour the game so, as an activity that can totally transcend other energy-sapping worries. The magic of card play is undeniable, but the real beauty of bridge for me, and the modern challenge, lies in the bidding. The potential for substantial improvement in performance also lies with optimum bidding effectiveness regardless of your present position on the bridge ladder.

I have been fascinated by bidding developments, played most bidding systems in three countries, taught bridge at advanced level, invented a few systems and sometimes wished the journey was not so lonely or frustrating. I concluded that, short of Mollo's nightmare of Tomorrow's Bridge being realised (viz. that we more or less told partner exactly what we had in each suit and bored the opposition's socks off in the process), the real deficiency of bidding lay not so much in the system but in its foundation, Hand Evaluation. However, as you will discover, I have some very strong views on traditional bidding methods too, which like the English language leave much to be desired.

In short, if we have struggled throughout the history of bridge to acknowledge, accept and use a hand valuation method that really works, it is not surprising that bidding systems let us down. I know personally, and read about frequently, many great card players whose bidding is unconvincing, pedestrian or stone age (or all three). I am left pondering this disparity between the two facets of this game, which seem to be so different in their intellectual demands, one (play) being mainly left-brained and mathematical, and the other (bidding) primarily right-brained and a creative language. Therein, undoubtedly lies the main basis for the game being impossible to completely master or mistress.

The other hurdle to overcome in presenting new evaluation and bidding ideas is the natural conservatism, resistance or mindset of human nature. Not only are many people essentially lazy but the idea of change is abhorrent simply because it inadvertently casts a blight on their previous position. But, more than that, when we have been inculcated with a particular bidding approach, it is really mind-bending to be confronted with something that breaks the previous rules; it is almost as if we get withdrawal symptoms without the security of our favourite tried and trusted, if not true, methods.

However, I will be an 'optimist for a change' fuelled by feedback from those who have drunk at the well, feel a little heady and never want to go back to being 'well less', although my mate Steve has said from time to time, 'Ooh me head hurts' after an intense session.

This book, originally entitled 'Beautiful Bidding', logically starts in Section 1 with hand valuation, introducing for the first time a new total dynamic concept, 'Complete Valuation' (CV).

Section 2 – in exploring the essential link between tricks and controls, shows how new thinking in this area automatically determines the quality, interpretation and application of any existing bidding system as well as being a cornerstone for revolutionising the design of futuristic systems.

Section 3 – heralds for the first time a bidding system, 'MIDMAC' which has all the hallmarks of optimising originality, simplicity and effectiveness. In short, it's a winner because it succeeds in producing incredibly accurate sequences in terms of describing strength and shape, with a minimum of fuss and retaining inherent naturalness. Because you can work out what to bid and what the meaning of a bid is, you do not have to remember codified responses to relays and you do not have long boring sequences that send the opponents into 'Z' land.

Finally, in Section 4 – Bidding Tips and Tops, the bidding connoisseur will be titillated by a fair sprinkling of bidding concepts which make the most of those special magic moments that can create the really big bidding swings.

So come fly with me, if you will. Dismiss, if you can, the nagging doubt of the sceptic; 'Jon who?' they will say, as a way of dismissing the possibility of taking on board something different especially advocated by an 'unknown'. 'He can't be any good because Reese, Belladonna or Zia haven't endorsed the book'. I will let you into a secret; I didn't ask these notables because I want you the reader to be your own judges. I sincerely hope you find your own journey as exciting and beautiful as mine has been. I am confident your game will get a totally new lease of life as your stunned opponents leave you with the parting 'I fear you bid well!'

Jon Drabble
August 1995

To my Step-father **Beezer**.

A beautiful man who struggled with life and death during much of the time this book was being prepared.

'With so much love to send you on your way.'

1
COMPLETE HAND VALUATION

Introduction

How many times have you heard the line ...

'We couldn't possibly bid game, partner, I knew we didn't have more than 22 points between us.' ... or ...

'We had to try for game because you opened the bidding and I had an opening bid too.'

Why is it that some deals produce no more than a part score whereas others yield a game or even a slam in both directions?

Something is obviously wrong somewhere when the sacred high-card point count (HCPC) lets us down so often. If you, and your partner, can regularly and reliably bid hands such as these two to game (4♠),

1. ♠ AJxx   ♠ K10xxx
    ♡ x      ♡ xxxx
    ◇ Kxxx   ◇ xx
    ♣ AJxx   ♣ Kx

despite there being only a combined HCPC of 19 ... and stay out of game (3NT) with:

2. ♠ Kxx   ♠ Qxxx
    ♡ Axx   ♡ Kxxx
    ◇ QJx   ◇ Axxx
    ♣ AQ10x   ♣ x

... despite there being a combined HCPC of 25 – then do not waste your time and energy further with my ravings about CV.

If, however, your bidding is not already so immaculate and you are intrigued enough to want to change, then you might be interested to know that CV values hand 1 at 27 and hand 2 at only 22.

The ingredient of bridge which is the cornerstone of successful bidding – optimum hand evaluation – is what this section is all about.

1.1 History of Hand Evaluation (HV)

Since Milton Work advanced his ideas to correct for fit his original 4-3-2-1 HCPC count in 1929, there have been many frustrated HV inventors, none more critical than the proud parent of Losing Trick Count (LTC) (1934), Dudley Courtenay, who referred to 'that atrocity – suit bidding via the 4-3-2-1 point count'. Twenty-seven years later in desperation he passed on all rights to LTC on to M. Harrison-Gray with 'the profound hope that in its resurrection you will have more success in making the heathen see the light than I did'. Such is the entrenchment of human nature, that even 60 years later nothing much has changed despite the best efforts of some pretty big guns:

1930s – Culbertson, Criticus and Bisset all proposed methods for improving hand evaluation, none of which gained any widespread acceptance because, as with Milton Work's first attempts, bridge players were, it seems, incapable of making all the necessary corrections at the table.

1940s and '50s – Counting distribution points became popular, thus was born the fairly well known 3-2-1 for voids, singletons and doubletons respectively. Fred Karpin and a Canadian, William Anderson, proposed some new ideas for further additions for hands with a fit. In fact Anderson's ideas were adapted by Goren and included in most of his successful books.

Meanwhile, Culbertson's swan song for bridge was the publication of a hand evaluation scheme which he recognised was what the public desperately wanted and needed; however, it was so complicated it did not gain general acceptance.

1960s and '70s – Al Roth and Jeff Rubens suggested variations on the Goren Point Count, but still the outcome was a vast array of tables involving corrections that players found too difficult to remember.

In 1976 Truscott devised his 'Ideal' distribution point count, which he called 'Assets' when writing about it 8 years later. The novelty of Assets deserves some amplification, so it is included as a footnote at the end of this section.

1980s and '90s – In 1983 John Graham felt that 'We teach bridge wrongly even to beginners'. He introduced a philosophy, rather than system, for hand valuation based on tricks not points and noted that hand valuation should be a composite of HCPC, distribution, fit and control. In 1983 a computer designed Bidding System, Cobra (Torbjorn Lindelof) introduced an unusually thorough although somewhat complex approach to Hand Valuation.

About the same time, Joe Amsbury recognised the enormous value of fit with his explosive TNT (Payne, R., and Amsbury, J. – *Bridge: TNT and Competitive Bidding*. Batsford, London 1981).

The Vernes Law on Total Tricks was also amplified by Larry Cohen in his book *To Bid or Not to Bid* in 1992, the only book exclusively covering TNT, and raising the 'Law' to God-like status!

Also in the nineties Ron Klinger and Hugh Kelsey have acknowledged the extra value of shape by suggesting a 5-3-1 addition for void-singleton-doubleton to replace the long standing 3-2-1.

Author's Comment

Both John Graham and Joe Amsbury/Dick Payne have had a large impact on me, and I gratefully acknowledge their contribution to my present thinking. I recall reading John Graham's article in Bridge Magazine, Nov. 1983, whilst living in New Zealand and thinking this fellow makes a lot of sense. I have John to thank for setting me on the way to CV.

Truscott's Asset idea (Bridge International, Sept. 1984), which I didn't know about when developing CV, offers much to supplement HCPC and is much easier for me than LTC. It's main flaws would appear to be that it undervalues hands with an 8 card or Moysian (4-3) fit and it overvalues hands involving misfits. Personally, I do not like the idea of another evaluation denomination (assets), as well as points, but I just might be biased.

In summary, this 64 year review of the history of hand valuation reveals, once again, that all we learn from history is that we do not seem to learn much from history. For those bridge players who share my view that the enormous potential of bidding is so often denied by inadequate hand valuation, welcome to the 21st century: for the rest, that's history.

1.2 Optimum Hand Valuation

Bidding is about three times more important than play at any level. As the standard of the contestants gets better it is bidding accurately to sensible contracts that determines the winners; this is primarily because there is little to choose between the contestants in card play.

Beginners and intermediate players often underbid and sometimes overbid, but even advanced players get it wrong. Why? You may well ask. I believe the answer is that at the lower levels there is a slavish fixation with high card point count and at higher levels there is a lack of something better that can be understood and regularly used as an adjunct or alternative.

High card point count (HCPC) is woefully inadequate for anything other than situations where both hands are balanced, whether a fit is available or not; this is another way of saying that high card point count is nothing like good enough on something like 90% of all hand combinations, since 85% of hands in combination have an eight-card (or better) fit and about 5% involve misfitting unbalanced hands.

Using distribution count to supplement HCPC comes to the rescue, in part, on some hands. Rather complex methods such as LTC ('Losing Trick Count') are available for the 'brain-drainers' on hands with a fit. The dynamic TNT (Total Number of Tricks) helps players realise the need to be aggressive when a fit has been diagnosed, both for tactical and constructive reasons; the corollary, to be cautious when the hands are misfitting and no 8+ card fit is available, follows naturally.

What is missing is a reliable, simple, consistent method of hand valuation suitable for all hands, whether they are balanced, unbalanced, involve fits or misfits or any combination thereof.

The good news is that complete hand valuation (CV) is now available, and it works. It will give a new lease of life to players at any level who feel their bidding accuracy leaves room for improvement, whether or not the opposition are getting into the act. Moreover, having started to use CV you can improve your results drastically regardless of your bidding systems and even if your partner has never heard of CV. Once both of you have assimilated the method, and it will not take very long, you will not need any other hand valuation supplements. As the name suggests CV is comprehensive and 'unabridged'!

The accuracy and efficiency of CV has been confirmed not just by personal experience but also by testing it on many thousands of hands from all sources including World Championship play. In one exercise looking at 100 particularly difficult hands used to promote a complex modified losing trick count method, the correlation between CV and ideal level of contract was 98%.

Read on you doubting Thomases. I believe you are in for a pleasant surprise.

1.3 Inadequacy of HCPC

It does not take a genius to realise that on hands where both sides can make a game, or even a slam, the number of high card points per pack has not magically increased. Since the HCPC per pack is (usually!) only 40, both sides cannot have 25+ or 30 plus each. Hence the correlation between HCPC and number of tricks available is clearly limited.

With CV there is no such problem since the aggregated valuation of all four hands in a deal is not fixed at 40 but can vary from less than 40 to more than 70. If you still have any doubt about the inadequacy of HCPC for accurate hand evaluation look at these two pairs of hands:

Hand 1.

♠ Ax		♠ KJ9xx
♡ Axxxxx	N	♡ x
◊ Qxxx	W E	◊ Kx
♣ x	S	♣ AJxxx

The combined HCPC = 22 and you will struggle to make any contract at the two level. 2♡ is as high as you would want to be.

Hand 2.

♠ Ax		♠ x
♡ Axxxxx	N	♡ KJ9xx
◊ Qxxx	W E	◊ Kx
♣ x	S	♣ AJxxx

The combined HCPC = 22 but now 6♡ is unbeatable.

A difference of four levels in the optimum contract simply by switching the major suits in East hand. Truly amazing? By the end of this section with CV to the rescue, you will be able to bid these hands accurately and confidently. In fact, the combined CV of hand 1 is coincidentally still 22 but for hand 2 is 35. How this works you will find out shortly.

1.4 Are You Ready for CV?

Bridge players are notorious for excusing technical deficiencies by thinking that they simply 'took a view' and sometimes the idea of a long-standing club player wanting or needing to improve seems totally unpalatable.

Are you open minded enough to admit that you have picked up some bad habits or abused some bridge maxims along the way which need correcting?

Do you want to improve your bidding dramatically and feature more frequently among the winners?

Are you prepared to discard some old ideas and try something new, despite your egocentricity?

Are you prepared to work really hard?

If the answer is yes to only three out of these four questions read on, otherwise put this book on to a shelf to gather dust, or preferably give somebody else the benefit who is prepared to decondition themselves.

Why do only three out of four questions need an affirmative? The good news is that CV is not difficult once you have mastered the rudiments of this wonderful game. However I recommend that you have played bridge for at least a year before taking up CV.

1.5 What is CV?

CV is a direct and accurate way of determining the number of tricks a hand can produce. The complete valuation of a hand is, or should be, a quantitative assessment which incorporates a composite of: high card points, distribution points, fit/misfit points and controls. It still involves the familiar point count for ease of assimilation.

Starting with the HCPC, calculated by the usual 4-3-2-1 for AKQJ respectively, add an extra 1 point for an excess of 10s and 9s, and deduct 1 point for each short suit (3 or less) containing exclusively honour cards. (AKQ or J).

Distribution Points (DP)

Distribution points take account of the fact that unbalanced hands are worth more than balanced hands for both offence and defence.

Completely flat hands (4-3-3-3 type) should therefore have a point deducted and all hands more distributional than the most common 4-4-3-2 and 5-3-3-2 types should have points added using the following easy to remember rule:

Unbalanced hands only: 5 or 4/4   +1 point
                          6 or 5/5   +2 points
                          7 or 6/6   +3 points

If you use this simple method for calculating DPs you will never be more than a point out, but, for those with a scientific bent and a capacity for exactitude and hard work, Table 1 gives the exact distribution point correction for all hand shapes based on a unique formula:

Distribution points (DP) are calculated by adding the two longest suits together, dividing the sum by three and subtracting the length of the shortest suit (rounding off downwards to whole numbers).

In all example hands throughout this book the refined exact distribution point correlation will be used as per Table 1.

Table 1 – Distribution for all Hand Patterns

Pattern	DP	Pattern	DP	Pattern	DP
4-3-3-3	−1	5-5-3-0	3	7-2-2-2	1
4-4-3-2	0	6-3-2-2	1	7-3-2-1	2
4-4-4-1	1	6-4-2-1	2	7-4-1-1	2
5-3-3-2	0	6-3-3-1	2	7-4-2-0	3
5-4-2-2	1	6-5-1-1	2	7-3-3-0	3
5-4-3-1	2	6-4-3-0	3	7-5-1-0	4
5-5-2-1	2	6-5-2-0	3	7-6-0-0	4
5-4-4-0	3	6-6-1-0	4		

More distributional patterns = 4 DP

Fit (and misfit) Points (FP)

Once the bidding is underway fit points come into consideration.

Fit points are calculated by:

Minimum 8 card fit   +3 pts = 1 trick
Minimum 9 card fit   +6 pts = 2 tricks
Minimum 10 card fit   +9 pts = 3 tricks

and beyond if you have sufficient controls (see Section 2 for amplification).

On the other hand, if you have a void or singleton spot card in partner's naturally bid suit you deduct 3 pts (1 trick) for the misfit, but experience has shown you do not downgrade for singleton A,K or Q.

Controls
Controls (A = 2, K = 1)

A hand with good controls should be bid more aggressively because controls are useful for both offence and defence. If CV is borderline, good controls should encourage a more optimistic decision for the next bid, and the converse applies for poor controls. If the control factor (CF), which is defined as 3 x number of controls divided by the HCP, is greater than 1 they are good. If the CF is less than 1 the controls are poor.

Tricks
The link between CV, controls and tricks will be explored fully in Section 2.

All this means that for initial hand valuation when considering your opening bid (or response to an artificial bid)

$$CV = HCP + DP$$

For hand valuation after your partner has already bid naturally (i.e. responses and rebids)

$$CV = HCP + DP + FP$$

It is CV that determines the bid at any point of the auction, not HCPC. CV is not fixed; it can go up down and frequently does, as the auction progresses. If you add your CV to the minimum shown by partner you know the minimum appropriate level of contract as indicated by the following CV requirements:

The Combined Complete Valuation (CCV) for various levels of contract (NT or Suit) is:

2 level	21-23	22±1	5 level	30-32	31±1
3 level	24-26	25±1	6 level	33-35	34±1
4 level	27-29	28±1	7 level	36+	

Note that CCV is so accurate that when greater than 40 it can tell you if you can make overtricks in a grand slam!

1.6 Link Between CV and Bidding System

Using Benjamised Acol as a base, the following section gives the CV requirements for opening bids, responses and rebids. The keen observer will note that perhaps other than suit raises the point requirements are similar to those you will already be familiar with, although we do keep our 2 over 1 responses strictly up to 10+ points so that we are guaranteed a CCV of 21+ for the two level bids.

Opening Bids	CV	Requirements
1 suit		11-20 (minimum of 3 controls if < 11HCP)
1NT		12-14 (CV = HCP for initial valuation)
2♣		21-23 or 8+ playing tricks major or 9+ playing tricks minor and minimum of 5 control if < 21 HCP)
2◇		23/24 +
2♡/2♠		6-10
3 suit		6-10 perhaps, up to 13 in 3rd position or if insufficient controls for a 1 suit opening

Responses	CV	Requirements		
1 over 1	6+	1NT	6-9	
2 over 1	10+	2NT	11-12	
Jump	16+			
2 level suit raise	6-10	4+ suit or 3 to honour and ruffing value		
3 level suit raise	11-12	4+ suit		
4 level suit raise	13-15	4+ suit		

Note if CV is 16+ including 8+ fit temporise by responding in a new suit

Opener's rebids	CV	Requirements
non forcing suit	11-16	
simple raise	14-15	
jump raise	17-19	
double jump raise	20- 21	
temporise	22+ (including fit)	
forcing reverse or jump new suit 18+		

Enough of the preamble and theory; let's see some action:

1.7 Examples of CV

Opening Bids:

♠ AQ9xxx   CV = 9 (HCP) +2 (DP) = 11. Fair CF
♡ x
◇ K10x
♣ 10xx

Since CV = 11+ (better than average spot cards) and there are sufficient controls (minimum of three (3) required for an opening 1 bid if less than 11 HCP) the opening bid should be 1♠.

♠ Axx   CV = 12 (HCP) –1 (DP) = 11. Poor CF
♡ K9xx
◇ Q8x
♣ QJx

Therefore pass or possibly open 1NT, in 4th position or 3rd position at favourable vulnerability.

♠ K1098x   CV = 11 (HCP inc. excess 10s etc) + 2 (DP) = 13.
♡ AJ10x   Poor CF
◇ Q108
♣ x

Therefore open 1♠.

♠ KQ   CV = 8 (HCP less 2 for short suits with honours)
♡ J8xxx   +2 (DP) = 10. Poor CF
◇ 10xxxx
♣ A

Therefore pass.

♠ AK109xxx   CV = 14 (HCP) +2 (DP) = 16. Very good CF
♡ x
◇ AKxx
♣ x

Open 2♣ holding 8 playing tricks in spades and more than 5 controls.

Responses

Partner opens 1♡ showing 4+ suit.

What do you respond with:

♠ x   CV = 9 (HCP) + 2 (DP) + 3 (FP) = 14. Fair CF
♡ A10xx
◊ KQ9xx
♣ xxx

Therefore raise to 3♡. CCV = 25+. (We will look at obstructive shaded raises in Section 4.)

Now let us see what happens when we exchange the major suits:

♠ A10xx   CV = 9 (HCP) +2 (DP) –3 (FP) = 8. Fair CF
♡ x
◊ KQ9xx
♣ xxx

Now, respond 1♠ to 1♡ opener (not strong enough for 2◊ response). Note this hand is worth a CV of six less than previous hand (2 tricks less) despite the same HCPC. Our CCV may be as little as 18.

♠ Qxx   CV = 10 (HCP) +2 (DP) –3 (FP) = 9. Poor CF
♡ x
◊ KQ10x
♣ K108xx

Therefore, respond 1NT. Remember that a 2 over 1 response strictly shows 10+ CV. On this hand CCV may not be more than 20 so you do not want to proceed to the 2 level.

♠ xx   CV = 9 (HCP) + (DP) = 10. Fair CF
♡ Kxx
◊ xx
♣ AQ10xxx

Here, we have enough to respond 2♣ and raise a 2♡ rebid to 3♡ because CV would then become 13 because of guaranteed minimum 8 card heart fit which would ensure a CCV of 24+, enough for the 3 level.

♠ x   CV = 14 (HCP) +2 (DP) +6 (FP) = 22. Good CF
♡ KQ10xx
◊ AJxxx
♣ Ax

Here we might temporise by responding 2◊ intending to look for 6 or 7♡ since CCV = 33+.

♠ x   CV = 8 +2 +3 = 13. Poor CF
♥ Qxxx
♦ Jx
♣ AJ9xxx

Therefore respond 3♥, CCV = 24+.

Rebids

Partner responds 1♠ (promising 4+ suit) to your opening 1♣ bid, what is your rebid?

♠ AJxx   Initial CV = 13 +2 = 15.
♥ x   New CV = 15 +3 (FP) = 18. Fair CF
♦ Kx
♣ KQ10xxx

We can raise partner's 1♠ response to 3♠ knowing minimum CCV is 24+ because 1♠ response promises 6+.

Partner raises your 1♥ opening to 2♥. What is your rebid?

♠ Axxx   Initial CV = 13 +2 = 15.
♥ AQ9xxx   New CV = 15 +6 (FP) = 21
♦ x   (because of 2 extra Trumps beyond those already
♣ Kx   promised). Excellent CF

Therefore rebid 4♥ since CCV is at least 27: in fact 27-31.

Partner responds 1♠ to your 1♣ opening. Over to you ...

♠ x   Initial CV = 13 +2 = 15. New CV = 15 –3 = 12
♥ AJxx   (because of spade misfit). Fair CF
♦ Kx
♣ KQ10xxx

Therefore, quietly rebid 2♣ since CCV could be as little as 18!

Partner responds 1♠ to your 1♥ opening. What now ...

♠ x   Initial CV = 16 +2 = 18. New CV = 18 –3 = 15.
♥ AK10xx   Very good CF
♦ Qx
♣ AKxxx

Therefore quietly rebid 2♣, not 3♣, since CCV could be as little as 21.

Partner responds 2♡ to your 1♠ opening. What is your choice of rebid?

♠ Axxxx   Initial CV = 12 +2 = 14. New CV = 13 +3 = 17
♡ Axx   because of 8+ card ♡ fit. Very good CF.
♢ x
♣ KJxx

So raise 2♡ response to 4♡ since CCV is 27 at least and all suits are controlled.

Before we look at some exciting full sequences you will already have realised that the minimum CCV indicated from the bidding at any particular point of the auction determines the suggested level of the contract and therefore the next bid. If the CCV is at or near the minimum of the 3 point range for a particular level then quality of controls, and perhaps positional values if opposition have bid, determine whether you proceed directly to that level.

If, on the other hand, the minimum CCV is clearly towards the upper end of the 3 point range and the control factor is good bid directly to the appropriate level, or if looking for slam check for controls using your normal methods and then go for the commensurate level contract if you do not have two quick losers (small slam) or one quick loser (grand slam).

In the following full sequences, CV is shown in parenthesis after each bid. Note how CV is dynamic, not constant.

			West	East
♠ AJ9xx		♠ xx	1♠(12)	2♡(10)
♡ KQ10x	N W E S	♡ A9xxx	4♡(18)	CCV = 28
♢ xxx		♢ xx		
♣ x		♣ AJxx		

			West	East
♠ AQ9xx		♠ 10x	1♠(19)	2♡(13)
♡ K10x	N W E S	♡ AJ9xx	3♣(22)	3♢(i)
♢ x		♢ AJxx	4NT(ii)	5♡(iii)
♣ AK10x		♣ Qx	5NT(iv)	6♣(v)
			6♡	CCV = 35

(i)   4th suit showing more than minimum
(ii)   Key Card Blackwood
(iii) 2 Key cards
(iv) King asking
(v)   No kings

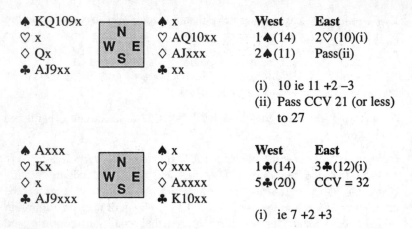

	♠ KQ109x	♠ x	**West**	**East**
	♡ x	♡ AQ10xx	1♠(14)	2♡(10)(i)
	◊ Qx	◊ AJxxx	2♠(11)	Pass(ii)
	♣ AJ9xx	♣ xx		

(i) 10 ie 11 +2 –3

(ii) Pass CCV 21 (or less) to 27

	♠ Axxx	♠ x	**West**	**East**
	♡ Kx	♡ xxx	1♣(14)	3♣(12)(i)
	◊ x	◊ Axxxx	5♣(20)	CCV = 32
	♣ AJ9xxx	♣ K10xx		

(i) ie 7 +2 +3

Note on this hand that the opposition actually have more HCP! The excellent controls of the West hand (LHS) make 5♣ a good shot when East shows CV of 11/12 with 4+ clubs.

	♠ x	♠ AJ98xx	**West**	**East**
	♡ A108x	♡ Jxx	1♣(18)	1♠(9)
	◊ KQxx	◊ Jx	1NT(15)	2♠(9)
	♣ AKJx	♣ 9x	Pass	CCV = 24

Now a pair of hands with competitive bidding from opponents.

East/West Game. Dealer East.

	♠ A10x	♠ QJ87xx
	♡ A9xxxx	♡ x
	◊ AK10	◊ xxx
	♣ x	♣ xxx

West	**North**	**East**	**South**
–	–	Pass	1♣
Dble(18)	Pass	1♠(5)	2♣
2♡(18)	3♣	3♠(5)	Pass
?			

East's bidding has shown 5+ spades, probably 6, and presumably a little bit of strength for the free 3♠ after the unencouraging initial forced response of 1♠. Therefore, by the third round of bidding the West hand has become worth a CV of 21, possibly 24. Having controls in every suit is superb, therefore knowing that CCV is near the minimum for the four level even if East has nothing more than 5 spades, West has a clearcut bid of 4♠. At the table 5♠ made despite the ♠K being offside by the expediency of establishing the heart suit for 2 minor suit discards.

'What's this?' say the opposition, 'Making 5♠ with only 18 HCP between them – is that allowed in the Green Book?'

Now look at a situation involving all four hands:

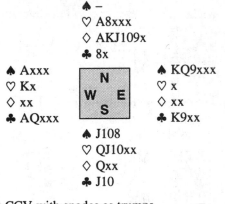

```
              ♠ –
              ♡ A8xxx
              ◇ AKJ109x
              ♣ 8x
  ♠ Axxx                    ♠ KQ9xxx
  ♡ Kx        N             ♡ x
  ◇ xx     W     E          ◇ xx
  ♣ AQxxx     S             ♣ K9xx
              ♠ J108
              ♡ QJ10xx
              ◇ Qxx
              ♣ J10
```

East/West CCV with spades as trumps	=	31
North/South CCV with hearts as trumps	=	32

Therefore, in a competitive auction both East/West and North/South should be bidding to the 5 level. Note that par should be 5♠ by East (doubled) which might even make if the defence try to take two heart tricks before cashing their two diamond winners.

Finally, note that CV can go up and down again (and vice versa) in the same auction.

```
  ♠ x                  ♠ AJxxx      West        East
  ♡ A10xx     N        ♡ Qxxx       1♣(18)      1♠(8)
  ◇ Axxx   W     E     ◇ xx         1NT(15)     2♡(8)(i)
  ♣ AKQx      S        ♣ xx         4♡(18)
```

(i)   non forcing

This hand also demonstrates the value of controls for aggressive bidding once a fit is found.

Parting Shot
No longer will you now be satisfied with your partner bleating *'We couldn't*

bid slam partner because I knew we only had 25 high card points, or so, between us.' Equally you will no longer be able to lament, using HCPC as the scapegoat.

Initially, using CV, it will be like driving a manual car after many years with an automatic; new awareness, excitement and a feeling of being in control. After a while it will become second nature as you use the method apparently automatically.

To return to the beginning, the two hands in the introduction will be easy fare for you now.

1. ♠ AJxx   ♠ K10xxx

♠ AJxx	♠ K10xxx	**West** **East**
♡ x	♡ xxxx	1♣(14) 1♠(7)
◇ Kxxx	◇ xx	3♠(17) 4♠(10)
♣ AJxx	♣ Kx	
		CCV = 27

2. ♠ Kxx	♠ Qxxx	**West** **East**
♡ Axx	♡ Kxxx	1♣(15) 1◇(7)
◇ QJx	◇ Axxx	1NT Pass
♣ AQ10x	♣ x	
		CCV = 22

CV proponents will find the game of bridge more digestible but CV opponents will be the ones with indigestion. I promise you, or as they say in the commercials, *'Or your money back'*.

It is suggested at this point you try out the CV method with hands from your other favourite bridge books, so that you develop as much faith in CV as its many disciples have done already.

1.8 Fine Tuning of CV

Although CV cannot diagnose the rare factors which condense the number of winners (any more than any other hand valuation method) such as:

Duplication of: • Hand Pattern • Controls • Values • Losers •

(you will need a relay bidding system to do that) – the method presented so far has been found to work well in excess of 95% of all hands. Extensive analysis can eliminate a few additional anomalies and these situations are revealed hereafter.

It may be as well that you only try and assimilate these additional points after using simple CV for a while.

1. Don't count both fit points and distribution points for hands where the fit suit is the only 4+ suit in the hand – count fit points only.

♠ x		♠ xxxx	**West** **East**
♡ AQ10xxx		♡ K9xx	1♡(14) 2♡(8)
◊ Kxx		◊ xx	3♡(18)(i) Pass
♣ Kxx		♣ Qxx	

CCV = 26
(i) 14 + 6 - 2

As the West hand is single suited, and that suit is the fit suit, DP is belatedly discounted.

Note that West's control factor is only fair (1) and it would be pushy to jump to 4♡ unless you sense you need to bid aggressively to stop opponents belatedly entering the auction. Since East may have a CV as little as 6, CCV may only be 24 so 3♡ is enough. Making either minor suit king an ace would be enough to tip the balance in favour of 4♡.

Note that, if 3♡ doesn't make with the above hands because the A◊ is over the K◊, it is a good (advanced) sacrifice against the opponents 4♠ which would then make.

2. If your hand is flat (4-3-3-3 type) do not count full value of fit points because there is no ruffing value. In fact discount one level of fit (3 points).

♠ AQ98xx		♠ Kxx	**West** **East**
♡ x		♡ K10xx	1♠(14) 1NT(9)
◊ AJ10		◊ 8xx	2♠(14)(i) 2NT(12)
♣ Jxx		♣ A9x	3◊(ii) 3NT
			CCV = 26

(i) Promises 6 spades
(ii) Not min.

The only logical explanation for this unusual responder's sequence is that the value of East's hand has increased based on a belated fit.

When CCV is 26 a three level game contract is usually easier than a four level game.

Note that, despite only 22HCP, 3NT is considerably better than 50%.

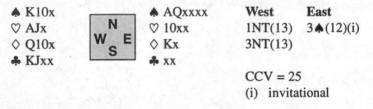

		West	East
♠ K10x	♠ AQxxxx	1NT(13)	3♠(12)(i)
♡ AJx	♡ 10xx	3NT(13)	
◊ Q10x	◊ Kx		
♣ KJxx	♣ xx		

CCV = 25

(i) invitational

East knows immediately that there is at least an 8 card spade fit so the hand is worth 9+3 fit points (12), s/he doesn't count DP as well though. West with the vital K♠ and a maximum has a go for the game at a level commensurate with CV of 24/25. Note that West doesn't add 3 fit points because the hand is flat.

3. When CCV is borderline, controls determine whether you go to the higher level or stay at the lower level.

		West	East
♠ x	♠ xxxx	1♡(15)	2♡(8)
♡ AQ10xx	♡ K9xx	4♡(18)	
◊ Axxxx	◊ xx		
♣ Kx	♣ Qxx		

CCV = 26

Here there is another suit (diamonds) as well as the fit suit (hearts) so both DP and FP are counted. Although CCV could be as low as 24, not only does West have an excellent control factor but all suits are controlled as well. Note also that unless hearts break 2-2, 4♠ may well be on for the opposition. Fortunately for you they are obviously not using CV as well! Frequently with CV, when fits abound, the optimum constructive bid also turns out to be the best tactical bid.

4. Beware of duplication of trump length in balanced hands.

♠ Ax	♠ KQx
♡ KQxxx	♡ Axxxx
◊ Axx	◊ xx
♣ Qxx	♣ Axx

CCV for these two hands is in fact 37 and yet even 6♡ is clearly impossible unless K♣ falls singleton. It is, I am afraid, a fact of life that nothing (even the wonderful CV) is perfect. Let this hand be a rare exception that proves the rule.

If your partner has indicated a balanced hand (no singleton or void) and you have a balanced hand with the only long suit being the trump support suit then please be cautious; CV seems to inexplicably overstate such hands. Discount 2 levels of fit viz 6 points to compensate. If the responding hand is semi balanced 2 5 4 2 discount 1 level of fit.

With fine tuning the previous hands would be bid:

$$1♡(15) \qquad 4♡(16) \qquad CCV = 31$$

Trump Bound

♠ A7432		♠ KQJ109	**West**	**East**
♡ K9	N W E S	♡ 854	1♠(i)	?
◇ KQ3		◇ 965		
♣ AQ4		♣ 83	(i) 5 card major	

East can see if West has 5+ spades to the ace that the QJ of spades are wasted, so East goes slowly discounting 2 rounds of fit for the balanced hand and only counting the K♠, bringing CV to all of 6 points and therefore only worth a raise to 2♠. An aggressive West will now find 3NT although strictly 2NT is the limit. Staying out of the game on this trump bound hand is a major feat of hand evaluation. Notice, for instance, what happens if you transfer the QJ of spades with two small hearts in the East hand to give:

♠ K10865
♡ QJ4
◇ 965
♣ 83

Now combined with the above West hand this East hand produces an excellent 4♠ or 3NT.

If you have problems with any other types of situation, please let me know directly or via the publisher. In the several years of its development I have only heard complaints from the opposition, but my shoulders are broad enough, so fire away.

To finish up this fine tuning section, three more hands to whet your appetite.

Firstly, a hand to incorporate all the fine tuning principles, about as complex a CV calculation as you will get:

♠ AJ10xx	♠ xxxx
♡ Axxx	♡ Kxx
◇ Ax	◇ Kxx
♣ xx	♣ Axx

1. West   East   **2.** West   East
   1♠(14)   1NT(9)   1♠(14)   2♠(9)
   2♡(14)(i) 3♠(12)   3♡(17)   4♠
   4♠

(i) non forcing

Note firstly that the CF for both hands is very good (much greater than 1), which is primarily why a CCV of 26 produces such a good four level contract.

In response East values the hand at 9(10 –1) because it is flat and there are no fit points either, assuming initially that 1♠ opener only promises 4. The possible responses are 1NT(1) or 2♠(2).

1. After 1NT response West goes quietly rebidding 2♡ but at the same time promising 5 spades. Now East can value the hand at 12 because of three fit points which justifies the game try with 3♠. West has no hesitation in accepting the strong invitation with more than minimum and such good controls.

2. After 2♠ response it is West's turn to add on three (3) fit points and make a long suit try with 3♡. East being maximum for previous bidding, and having great controls and a key card in the secondary suit (hearts) is happy to push to game.

Now take a hand from the TNT Book.

East/West Game. Dealer North.

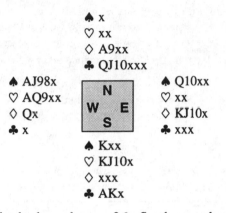

```
              ♠ x
              ♡ xx
              ◇ A9xx
              ♣ QJ10xxx
  ♠ AJ98x        ┌─────┐        ♠ Q10xx
  ♡ AQ9xx        │  N  │        ♡ xx
  ◇ Qx        W  │     │  E     ◇ KJ10x
  ♣ x            │  S  │        ♣ xxx
                 └─────┘
              ♠ Kxx
              ♡ KJ10x
              ◇ xxx
              ♣ AKx
```

If North is a little cheeky and opens 3♣, South can value the hand at 19 (14-1+6) or 16 if he knows his partner takes liberties! With such wonderful help in clubs a bid of 3NT closes the auction and NS will probably go one off on a major suit lead, with chances of sneaking the contract if West feels under pressure and gets end played.

Nothing remarkable about all that, you may say, but let's suppose North is not red-blooded and quietly passes. Now West makes some sort of major suit takeout noise over South's 1NT opening and raises East's 2♠ to 3♠, which East completes to game level.

CCV for EW is 19 (HCP)+2DP(W)+6FP which equals 27. Surprise, surprise, game makes, maybe with an overtrick on best declarer play.

CV is useful for competitive bidding too. If your partner, bless his cotton socks, makes a weak jump overcall of 2♠ over opponent's 1♡ opening and you are looking at:

```
              ♠ Axxx
              ♡ xxx
              ◇ x
              ♣ QJ9xx
```

When you hear or see right hand opponent leap to 4♡, what do you do?

Well, assuming partner has 6-10 points, 6 spades and poor defence (1 trick at most usually), it looks with your possible 2 tricks that opponents will make 4♡. Your CV is 18 (7 HCP +2 DP +9 FP). This little hand has almost tripled in its value in view of partner's 2♠ overcall!

If partner is minimum your CCV is 24 and all things being equal you will make nine tricks. If partner is maximum your CCV is 28 and you may well make 4♠. Either way CV tells you it is absolutely correct to bid 4♠ at any vulnerability. A typical middle-of-the-road non-vulnerable 2♠ jump overcall is:

    ♠ QJ10xxx   Note 4♠ is a 50% contract or thereabouts and the
    ♡ x   opposition can make at least 5♡.
    ◇ xxx
    ♣ Kxx

> *'Go forth, take your CV with you*
> *and before long you will come first.'*

Footnote; Assets à la Truscott

One adds Assets or distributional points to the HCPC according to the following scheme:

5 card or longer suit	1 Asset
Singleton	1 Asset
Void	2 Assets

When a fit is diagnosed for suit contracts a distributional correction was to be made by both players at each stage depending on the extent of known minimum fit.

Known fit	**Asset**
8 cards	no change
9 cards	double
10 cards	triple
no 8 + fit	ignored

Truscott gave as an example:

Partner has opened 1♡ promising at least 5 hearts and you have:

    ♠ x   You have three assets 2 x 5 card suits and one singleton.
    ♡ Kxxxx
    ◇ xx
    ♣ Jxxxx

Because you have at least a ten card fit you triple your three assets to 9 giving you a total valuation of 4 (HCP) +9 = 13, quite enough to raise 4♡.

If, on the other hand, partner had opened 1♠ (as my partner usually would!), now because there is no 8+ card fit in sight all assets are ignored, the valuation of the hand remains at 4 and you would not respond.

2
BIDDING: THE LANGUAGE OF BRIDGE

Introduction

Bidding is a language, the language of bridge. We have already looked at the alphabet, the hand valuation units. The available bids 1♣ –> 7NT as well as pass, double or redouble, provide the vocabulary whilst the bidding system is the particular language with say, for instance, 'Benjy' Acol being a sort of dialect of *Acol*.

During this section we will see that some languages are richer and more effective than others and to be effective the bidding language needs to be logical, consistent, easy to learn and retain and be based on sound hand valuation.

When bidding at bridge we are, as with any language, trying to communicate and thoroughly understand each other. What is it though that we are primarily trying to say? Well, we are trying to suggest to partner a level and denomination of contract related to the trick potential of the two combined hands (constructive bidding). However, at the same time we are also trying to stop the opponents from doing the same thing as effectively as we are (obstructive bidding). The 'cut and thrust' of bidding is that they, of course, are trying to do the same thing. In other words, as well as both the competing partnerships having an optimum constructive language they are sometimes trying to obstructively jam or distort their opponent's language so that it sends wrong messages; both partnerships knowing which mode, constructive or obstructive, they are using at any time is paramount for partnership understanding.

When we talk about level of contract or strength of hand this is only really symbolic for defining the number of available tricks in the combined hands or single hand respectively. This most important aspect – 'tricks' and how they relate to CV and controls – will be dealt with firstly because this is, or should be, the common ingredient for any bidding language or system. The difference between inferred tricks, playing tricks and quick tricks will also be spelt out.

Thorough partnership understanding of their chosen particular bidding language is essential for optimum communication. Although this simple, but often elusive, observation cannot be over-emphasised, a controversial theme will be developed that suggests that some traditional bidding approaches, such as Acol, are technically deficient, unsound and no longer ideal for modern teams bridge at the top. This is partly due to inadequate trick assessment (hand evaluation) but primarily because, in an attempt to make some of the doubtful initial concepts work, the bidding system has become cluttered, unwieldly, non-standardised and increasingly complex. In short Acol with all its necessary add-on bits is no longer logical, consistent and easy to remember, but played in its original form is simply not effective enough. Additionally, the indoctrination created by excessive focus on one bidding language and upheld by history, tradition and bureaucracy will be shown to have created mindsets which make it difficult, but fortunately not impossible, to objectively view or try other bidding methods, or in other words to progress.

2.1 Tricks of the Trade

You will already, having started to take on board CV, be finding that you are bidding more aggressively when you have a fit and more cautiously when you have a misfit. This will no doubt have improved your results greatly. For instance:

Game All. Dealer East.

♠ 7		♠ AQ843	West	East
♡ KQ652	N	♡ 98	–	Pass
◊ A2	W E	◊ 8742	1♡(17)	1♠(8)
♣ AQ843	S	♣ J7	2♣(14)	2♡
			Pass	

Appreciating the misfitting nature of these hands with a CCV of 22, 2♡ is surely as high as you would get, or want to be. In the 1986 World

Championship final one pair bid constructively to 3♡ and the other 'excelled' themselves by getting to 3NT. 3♡ was lucky enough to make with both black kings right for declarer and hearts and clubs breaking 3-3. 3NT, despite such favourable distribution, still deservedly went one off. No, this wasn't at the latter desperate stages of the match, it was only Board 20 out of the 128 board Final. Note, incidentally, that 14 out of 15 'big' swings in this final were due to bidding. The one above was only one of the 'small' ones.

You already also realise that the control factor is important, but no doubt it still seems rather nebulous and obscure trying to work out the trick taking potential of one hand, never mind two in combination.

This section Tricks of the Trade, is all about the rather difficult, and sometimes seemingly theoretical business of demystifying and objectifying tricks, the tools of the bidding trade. Of course it is easy when you can actually arithmetically count playing tricks on occasional hands like this:

			West	East
♠ xx		♠ KQxx	2♡	4♡
♡ AKQJ109x	N W E S	♡ xx		
◇ A		◇ xx		
♣ xxx		♣ Axxxx		

West promises 8 playing tricks. East counts 2 quick tricks, does a quick addition and comes up with 10 tricks, hence bids 4♡.

Sadly, on most hands the trick value of a hand is not obtainable so directly. For instance, what is the trick taking potential of this average undistinguished hand?

♠ KJ8x
♡ Q9xx
◇ A10xx
♣ x

The aim of this section is to be able to assign trick value to all hands and to convey the message of number of tricks in one hand to partner during the bidding, surely the 'bottom line' essence of any effective bidding language.

Link between CV, Tricks and Controls

We already know from Section 1 that for two hands in combination the link between CCV, level of contract and tricks (CT). We can add from statistical evidence the ideal and minimum number of controls associated with each level of contract to produce:

Table 2 – CV, Tricks and Controls (Combined Hands).

Contract Level	Combined Tricks	CCV±1	Ideal Controls	Minimum Controls
1	7	19	5	4
2	8	22	6	5
3	9	25	7	6
4	10	28	8	7
5	11	31	9	8
6	12	34	10	9
7	13	37	11	10

When we look at a similar table for single hands whereby *'1 Trick is equivalent to 3CV'* we produce:

Table 3 – CV, Tricks and Controls (Single Hands)

Contract Level	Tricks	CV±1	Typical Controls
	1	3	0
	2	6	1
	3	9	2
	4	12	3
	5	15	4
	6	18	5
1	7	21	6
2	8	24	7
3	9	27	8
4	10	30	9
5	11	33	10
6	12	36	11
7	13	39	12

You will note that: *'The number of controls should typically be within one less than the number of tricks for single hand evaluation.'*

The slight discrepancy between single and combination Tables 3 and 2 is due to:

1. Synergistic effect – two hands in combination sometimes produce up to 1 trick more than the sums of trick taking potential of single hands.

2. The single hand Table 3 is based on conservative assessment of trick taking potential, whilst for hands in combination we realistically need to be bidding hands to game or slam level which have as little as approximately 38%+ chance of success, depending on the bonuses for various levels and denominations with vulnerability. The actual chosen opening lead also sometimes improves that contract's chances considerably. For instance:

East/West Game. Dealer West.

    ♠ 83   ♠ K107
    ♡ AK9   ♡ Q84
    ◇ AKQ9643   ◇ 52
    ♣ 8   ♣ AQ965

The par contract 6NT (East), although not achieved by any pair in the 1989 World Championship, is in theory something like 50% since it makes (assuming no 4-0 diamond split) on either black suit finesse being successful. However, an opening black suit lead gives the contract away immediately and a non-black suit lead creates various inferences rather like 'the dog that didn't bark at night'. Even without this assistance or clue the optimum practical play is to play confidently and early towards the unsupported ♠K and even if the ♠A is wrong it requires an immediate spade return to kill 6NT. On any other red suit return (most likely a club!) you still have the contract in the bag if ♣K is right. So all in all, the practical chance for 6NT is well in excess of 75% even though the theoretical chance was 50% or less. So, all this means that the single hand Table 3 is theoretical whilst the combination Table 2 is practical, taking into account the rules and objectives of the game.

The difficulty of linking controls with trick potential (CV) is that, as we have seen, trick potential is dynamic for single hands depending on fits and/or misfits but the actual number of controls is fixed in a single hand whether or not we include shortage as well as Honour (Ace and King) controls. Ideally then, for constructive bidding it is the correlation between tricks/CV and controls that is important, not strictly the link between controls and HCP. In other words, the control factor should also become a variable as the bidding progresses.

The good news is that *'when a fit is determined shortage controls can be counted'*, so effectively the control factor is sometimes able to change alongside the number of tricks, the balance of tricks with controls remaining unaffected. Take this simple responding hand (West) as an example:

		CV	Tricks	Controls
♠ Kxx	Initial	10	3	3
♡ x	(1)	13	4	4
◇ Axxx	(2)	7	2	3
♣ Jxxxx				

(1) Partner opens 1♠ promising 5+ suit and 4+ tricks and you have ample to respond 2♠ (equivalent to 8 combined tricks). In fact, with the fit the responding hand is now worth 1 extra trick and there is also 1 extra control (heart singleton) which keeps trick/control ratio at unity. In short, there are enough tricks and controls to make a constructive 3♠ response because West can 'see' a minimum of 8 combined tricks and controls are one more than typical for the 4 trick West hand (CCV =24+)

(2) Partner opens 1♡, as partners do, and now CV falls by 1 trick so the West hand cannot even constructively bid higher than the one level because you may have as little as 6 tricks between you.

If we change the responding hand slightly:

West		CV	Tricks	Controls
♠ Kxxx	Initial	11	4	3
♡ -	(1)	17	6	5
◇ Axxx				
♣ Jxxxx				

(1) Partner, God bless him/her, opens 1♠ and the West hand is worth a genuine 4♠ because opener's 4 tricks with responder's 6 tricks come to 10. Note how, by counting 2 controls for the ♡ void, controls have matched tricks as they increased by 2 for two rounds of fit.

Before looking at two hands in combination, let us first recap on the three maxims that we use for single hand trick evaluation.

(1) 1 Trick = 3CV.

(2) Number of controls should be within one less than number of tricks.

(3) When a fit is determined shortage controls can and should be included.

Using these three maxims let us look at two hands in combination and see how both members of the partnership have their reckoning affected as they get new information from their partner.

Appearing Trick

You (West) open 1♣ with:

		CV	Tricks	Controls
♠ Axxx	Initial	12	4	5
♡ x	(a)	15	5	6
◇ Kxxx				
♣ Axxx				

(a) you gladly hear/see 1◇ response and rebid 1♠ which is followed by responder's 2♠ raise. What do you do? Well partner's mildly invitational 2♠ shows a hand willing to play at 8 trick level assuming you are a minimum 4 trick hand. Your CCV looks borderline for 4 level (26-28) so it looks like you do not have enough to go to 4♠ yourself. Is it worth making a game try? Controls should be looked at next – you have 6 controls including heart shortage which is 2 more than nominal for a 5 trick hand so that's excellent and therefore you invite further with 3◇.

Now over to responder (East) who is looking at:

East		CV	Tricks	Controls
♠ Kxxx	Initial	12	4	4
♡ Kxx	(i)	9	3	4
◇ A109xx	(ii)	12	4	5
♣ x				

(i)   After 1♣ opener
(ii) After 1♠ rebid

Responder, although only having 4 tricks, also has good controls (you shouldn't count the shortage control in partner's primary suit though), 1 more than nominal, so East goes for gold with 4♠.

The two hands together with tricks in parenthesis with + or – suffix to indicate good or bad controls

♠ Axxx		♠ Kxxx	West	East
♡ x	N	♡ Kxx	1♣(4++)	1◇(3++)
◇ Kxxx	W E	◇ A109xx	1♠(5++)	2♠(4++)
♣ Axxx	S	♣ x	3◇	4♠
			CCV 27	

If you look at combined tricks you only have 5 (West) + 4 (East) = 9. However, the controls are so good that they produce an extra trick apparently from nowhere to make the 10 trick game a good proposition. Let us now look at the converse:

Disappearing Trick
You (West) with :

		CV	Tricks	Controls
♠ Axxxx	Initial	14	5	3
♡ Qx				
◇ KQJ				
♣ QJx				

Open 1♠ promising 5+ and your partner raises constructively to 3♠ promising 5 tricks opposite your minimum of 4. You seem to have 10 tricks between you, so do you accept the invitation to 4♠? Well, you definitely wouldn't with an ordinary 4 trick hand but you do just have a 5 trick hand. What about controls? You do not have your nominal 4+ controls for a 5 trick hand so caution is called for and you proudly pass. The two hands in combination:

♠ Axxxx		♠ Qxxx	West	East
♡ Qx	N W E S	♡ Kxxx	1♠(5-)	3♠(5)
◇ KQJ		◇ x	Pass(i)	
♣ QJx		♣ Axxx		
			CCV 30	

    (i)   You might, as opener, consider 3NT if you move at all.

Justify your fine judgement despite CCV of 30.

So this time a trick seemed to disappear by virtue of poor controls. Note that, with ◇Axx instead of ◇KQJ, CV would be 1 less and controls 1 more and 4♠ would be a fine contract. All this confirms the fourth and final maxim that:

4. *'The quality of controls can affect the final outcome within a ± trick'*, which proves that whatever maxims you try to develop to help with bidding judgement, there is no substitute for 'thinking' to fine tune your subsequent action.

Now try this one yourself.

You open 1♠ with this hand:

(a)
                    ♠ Axxxx
                    ♡ Kxx
                    ◇ x
                    ♣ Axxx

and partner responds 2♡ promising 5+ hearts and CV 10+ (close to 4+ tricks). What do you do? Remember the four maxims for trick evaluation? When you have made your mind up, try the same process with this hand (b) after the same auction:

                    ♠ KJxxx
                    ♡ Qxx
                    ◇ x
                    ♣ KQJx

		CV	Tricks	Controls
For hand (a)	Initial	13	4++	5
	Final	16	5++	6

Because your controls are phenomenal (2 better than trick valuation) and all suits are controlled, you raise all the way to 4♡ which is a 1 trick upgrading.

		CV	Tricks	Controls
For hand (b)	Initial	14	5--	2
	Final	17	6--	3

After the same auction you only rebid 3♡ because controls are so poor despite appearing to have 10 tricks in combination.

The hands in combination:

Hand (a)	**Opener**	**Responder**
	♠ Axxxx	
	♡ Kxx	
	◇ x	
	♣ Axxx	♠ xx
		♡ Axxxx
Hand (b)	♠ KJxxx	◇ AQxx
	♡ Qxx	♣ xx
	◇ x	
	♣ KQJx	

You can work out for yourself the chances of 4♡ making with hands (a) and (b). I reckon with hand (a) it's about 50%, but with hand (b) about 25%.

Link between Tricks and Level of Bid

'The ideal bidding system should have openings, responses and rebids designed to promise a minimum number of tricks and the constructive bidding should not proceed beyond the level determined by the combination of tricks (CT) in both hands.'

A lofty ideal perhaps, but how do we set about achieving it?

To start with, Tables 2 and 3 with the subsequent four maxims derived within this section 2.1 should be the foundation for the optimum bidding system based on tricks. It should be structured in increments of 3CV (1 trick) with particular trick potential for all opening bids, primary constructive responses and rebids.

Opening Bids

It should all start with simple 1 suit openers which promise 4+ tricks (3 + HCP controls) based on the average reasonable expectation that partner's hand will have at least 3+ tricks unless subsequent bidding proves otherwise. Hence, if you have 4 tricks the remaining 9 tricks can be initially assumed to be divided 3 tricks each between the other 3 players giving you a fair chance for a one level or 7 trick contract. Simple openers would cover 4-6 trick hands which can be shown in 1 trick increments by subsequent graduated bidding. Stronger openers would take off from 7+ tricks.

Responses

2 or 3 tricks are enough to make a response which keeps the bidding open at the one level or simply raises opener's natural suit to the two level but to make a new suit forcing response at the two level responder should have close to 4+ tricks (combined CV of at least 21).

Opener's Rebids

If you have already opened the bidding 1 suit and heard partner make a one over one response showing 2+ tricks, you need 6+ tricks to jump the bidding to the three level and similarly 5+ tricks to move to the three level after a two over one response.

Complete Auction

The actual level of bid made by opener and responder at each turn is indicative of how many tricks they have in combination with the minimum promised by partner's previous bidding.

This sort of approach would lead to self explanatory auctions which get much closer to the playing trick example at the beginning of this section. For instance:

West	North	East	South
1♡	Pass	2♡	Pass
3♡	Pass	4♡	All Pass

Clearly means that opener has close to 7 tricks and therefore must have an extra heart or two. Responder must have 3 tricks. Both should have enough controls associated with their trick rating viz West 6+ controls and East 2+ controls – 'Simply beautiful and beautifully simple, is it not?'

Putting it all Together

If hand valuation is the alphabet of bidding language with HCP the vowels, then distribution, fits/misfits and controls are all very important consonants which go towards spelling out the CV which in turn is only a code for working out trick taking potential (1 inferred trick = 3CV). Once we have evaluated the initial CV of a single hand but before we have a chance to learn about fits or misfits after the auction has commenced, we can simply divide CV by three and convert the valuation into tricks. Thereafter, the value of the hand will only go up, or down, in multiples of 3x CV or 1 inferred trick. As the trick taking potential of a hand goes up with each level of fit all that remains before making the appropriate level of bid is to check that controls, including shortage, are commensurate with the new number of inferred tricks; that is, within one less than the number of tricks. If controls are much better than they need to be, you can show controlled aggression by upgrading 1 trick or 1 bidding level or be cautious and downgrade by 1 trick or 1 bidding level with very poor controls.

Take this simple hand with tricks in parenthesis. Note the suffix can be + or - or even ++ or --, indicating more or less controls than the nominal for that number of tricks.

♠ QJxx		♠ K9xx	West	East
♡ 9xx	**N**	♡ AKJx	1♣(4)	1♡(4+)
◇ Qx	**W E**	◇ xxx	1♠	3♠(5)
♣ AKJx	**S**	♣ 9x	?	

East has a clear 5 trick hand with typical 4 controls so is perfectly placed to rebid at the 4 + 5 = 9 level. Spotlight on West who has a little more than an absolute minimum. Can the West hand be pushed to 5 tricks to justify making a game bid. West checks controls and sees only 3 – not enough for a 5 trick hand. Qx is also a doubtful asset in a suit unbid by partner. So the answer is a definite 'NO'. Now change the West hand to one with the same CV:

♠ QJxx
♡ 9xx
◇ Kx
♣ AK10x

This would swing the decision towards 4♠ especially in teams just because of the extra control. You may well still pass in a pairs event because you know it will be tight.

Changing the ◇ Kx to ◇ Ax and you would bid 4♠ automatically in any event, because now you would have 5 tricks with 5 controls, 1 more than nominal.

Try another hand, playing 5 card majors:

♠ AJ108xx		♠ K9x	West	East
♡ x		♡ Axxx	1♠(5+)	2♠(3+)
◇ Kxxx		◇ xx	3◇(6+)	4♠
♣ AJ		♣ xxxx		

West can upgrade with extra trump length by a further trick counting heart shortage and so still maintaining good controls, invites naturally. East with 3 tricks and 1 extra control has an easy decision to accept the game suggestion; such is the approach for bidding thin games at teams.

We need Controls as well as Potential Tricks

East/West Game. Dealer West.

♠ QJ109xx		♠ xxx	West	East
♡ KJ		♡ Qx	Pass(4-)	1♣(4)
◇ 108		◇ AJ	2♠	Pass(5)
♣ K32		♣ AQ9876		

The West hand does not have the required 3 HCP controls for opening with a 1 bid (4+ trick hand) which is light in HCP so West makes a disciplined pass. Now East is perfectly placed to pass the 2♠ jump response knowing that they are unlikely to have more than 6 controls between them (remember you need a minimum of 7 for 10 trick contracts) Note that, playing weak twos in the majors, if West opens 2♠ East should still pass for the reason that 2♠ usually denies 3+ HCP controls.

It is a curious observation that with these two black suit fit hands East/West can actually make 12 tricks, but that is only after North/South have made their 4 tricks first. Who said there are only 13 tricks in a deal!? In this deal there seem to be 16! This is a frequent effect when controls do not match (are less than) potential tricks.

Some Oddities in Evaluating Shortage Controls

Sometimes when HCP controls match shortage controls in the same suit you get some interesting effects. Compare these two pairs of hands:

West		East	
♠ 3		♠ K98	CCV 29
♡ AK73	N	♡ J984	CT 10
◊ 10643	W E	◊ AQ752	CC 8
♣ KQJ8	S	♣ 5	

West	North	East	South
1♣(5)	Pass	1◊(3+)	Pass
1♡(6)	Pass	2♡(4)	Pass
4♡	All Pass		

All things (CCV, CT and CC) point to 4♡ being a fine contract and indeed most pairs would reach 4♡ readily enough. In fact the contract is borderline and not hopeless and if you never bid any worse than this you would be doing well.

Nevertheless, it is disappointing and surprising that 4♡ is not a better proposition, so what has happened?

Unfortunately, when shortage (singletons in the black suits) clash with the same value HCP control, i.e. A v void (2 v 2) or K v singleton (1 v 1), the value of the controls is offset by duplication.

West		East	
♠ 3		♠ A82	CCV 27
♡ AK73	N	♡ 10984	CT 10
◊ 10643	W E	◊ AQ752	CC 11
♣ A832	S	♣ 5	

West	North	East	South
1♣(4++)	Pass	1◊(3++)	Pass
1♡(5++)	Pass	3♡(4++)	Pass
3♠*	Pass	4♣(i)	Pass
4♡	All Pass		

(i)   Cuebids (1st or 2nd round)

Hand shapes for both opening and responding hands are identical for the two pairs of hands, and again 4♡ should be readily reached. This time though, 4♡ is almost frigid, 5♡ optimum with even 6♡ having some slight chance with diamonds becoming reserve trumps on an ideal break with ◊ K finessable. All this is primarily because combined controls (CC) are 11 and in both black suits the duplication of controls (shortage v HCP) no longer exists. In fact control matching (A v singleton or 2 v 1) is what you want to see and is only surpassed by optimum matching (0 HCP v void) as in the following hand which makes a complete mockery of HCP.

♠ AK109xx		♠ QJ87xx	CCV 35
♡ -	N	♡ xxxxx	CT 12+
◊ xxxxx	W E	◊ —	CC 9
♣ Ax	S	♣ xx	HCP 14

Ideal Bidding (5 card majors) :

West	North	East	South
1♠(5+)	Pass	4♠(5--)	Pass
5♣(6++)	Pass	5◊	Pass
5♡	Pass	5♠	Pass
6♠	All Pass		

(The opposition have obviously gone to sleep!)

Note that although combined controls (CC) are absolutely minimum for a 12 trick contract, 6♠ is 'icy'.

CCV is 35, if you count all 5 levels of fit and 6 for distribution to add to the mere combined 14 HCP.

It is interesting to reflect that the trick taking potential of this hand is almost 3 times that indicated by HCP. It is only CCV, and its related CT which comes somewhere near the mark in terms of predicting the optimum level of contract.

Now it is your turn:

Bidding Quiz 1 –
Bidding Practice (Tricks/Controls)

Bid these hands with your favourite method and assign inferred trick value based on appropriate minimum controls for each stage of the auction. Assume you and opponents are vulnerable and playing teams (IMP scoring) and the opponents do not bid, hence you are always bidding constructively.

Answers using 'Benjy' Acol are in Appendix 1.

1. ♠ K9	♠ Axxx	7. ♠ J108x	♠ 9
♡ AK87x	♡ 10xx	♡ KQJ109	♡ Axx
◇ x	◇ 98xx	◇ 8x	◇ A10xxx
♣ AQ9xx	♣ Kx	♣ Kx	♣ AJ10x
2. ♠ AJ98765	♠ Qxxx	8. ♠ KQ8x	♠ A9xx
♡ x	♡ A9xx	♡ Qx	♡ J108xx
◇ Axxx	◇ 98	◇ KJ9x	◇ xx
♣ x	♣ xxx	♣ AJ8	♣ Q10
3. ♠ KJ8765	♠ Qxxx	9. ♠ x	♠ A987x
♡ Qx	♡ A9xx	♡ KQJx	♡ 9x
◇ AQ	◇ 98	◇ Ax	◇ 98x
♣ QJ8	♣ xxx	♣ AQxxxx	♣ K10x
4. ♠ KQ	♠ xxx	10. ♠ AQ8	♠ J109
♡ 10xxx	♡ AJ9xx	♡ AKJx	♡ 109xx
◇ A109x	◇ xx	◇ 98xxx	◇ Ax
♣ AQx	♣ Kxx	♣ x	♣ Axxx
5. ♠ Qxxx	♠ AK10xx	11. ♠ AQJxx	♠ 8x
♡ AKQx	♡ Jx	♡ Q108	♡ KJx
◇ x	◇ 10xx	◇ K9	◇ QJxx
♣ AJ9x	♣ K8x	♣ 98x	♣ QJxx
6. ♠ KJ987x	♠ 10xxx	12. ♠ x	♠ A10
♡ Ax	♡ K10xx	♡ A10xxx	♡ Kxx
◇ AKQx	◇ 8x	◇ Q10x	◇ AKJxx
♣ J	♣ 10xx	♣ KJ9x	♣ A10x

Playing Trick (p.t.) Hands

As we have been exploring the rather seemingly nebulous factor of inferred tricks, with appropriate controls, from the foundation of CV and no doubt wishing it was all less painstaking, it will be a relief to recall that certain hands do not need this multiple translation but the trick-taking value is visibly self-evident from examination of the hand. You will notice also that these hands are usually single or two suited with most of the HCP in the long suits:

♠ xx
♡ KQJ109xx
◇ x
♣ Axx

Clearly this hand has 7 playing tricks provided it is played in hearts.

♠ KQJ10x
♡ xx
◇ KQJ98
♣ x

And this one has 7-8p.t.s provided it is played in spades or diamonds.

Hands with direct playing trick assessment such as these are often also conspicuous by virtue of:

- poor or limited defensive prospect because control to trick ratio is low.

- fair to useless unless played in the long suit/s (or occasionally no trumps if partner has the key filler/s and definite stoppers in other suits).

- poor correlation between CV and tricks for single hand evaluation.

- partner is more interested in quick tricks when responding to playing trick type hands to determine CT.

Game All. Dealer West.

West opens traditional 3♣ promising 6-7p.t.s East has 3½ quick tricks and with the key ♣K envisages 9 tricks on any lead therefore confidently responds 3NT. (A point here is that it makes good sense especially vulnerable in 1st and 2nd bidding position to have your pre-empts with most of strength in the long suit so that partner can judge whether to move or not.)

East can see on this hand that an 11 trick contract (5♣) is not a viable alternative, from the view point of both combined CV and controls.

So the conclusion is that, for accurate assessment of single constructive hands, CV and controls to give inferred tricks is essential but for single playing trick type hands which can have their trick-taking potential assessed directly, this approach is unnecessary. However, you will note that with such hands in combination CCV and CT still comes near the mark because of the extra tricks produced by the fit in the long suit.

An ideal bidding system therefore needs to differentiate clearly opening bids and responses which are obstructive and/or specifically descriptive in terms of playing tricks from those which are constructive and have an inferred trick value. In short, the previous hand should be able to be reliably and consistently bid to 3NT regardless of whether East or West happen to open the bidding. Sections 3 and 4 will show you how this can be arranged easily.

Constructive v Obstructive Bidding
Finally in this section, Tricks of the Trade, we need to recognise that so far we have been bidding without opposition intervention almost as if we do not have opponents or we are involved in a Bidding Challenge. Reality is something else because on typically half or more of the hands when we finish up declaring the final contract the opposition have said more than pass a few times. Opposition intervention is a mixed blessing but the fact is that as soon as they do interfere, or are threatening to, the luxury of your bids remaining entirely constructive is not realistic. Your bidding system should be most explicit about when your bidding is strictly constructive and when it is not. In other words, at which point does the priority of a bid need to shift focus towards making life difficult, if not impossible, for the opposition (obstructive or tactical bidding)?

I think the rules to answer this question are for once clearcut:

1. When the opponents have already interfered with a bid.

2. When the opponents have not yet interfered but your L.H. opponent has not already passed. That is to say you are responding or considering opening in third bidding position.

Whilst combined tricks (CT) with appropriate combined controls (CC) is the sure way for constructive bidding, when bidding obstructively particularly when raising opener's suit with a fit, combined tricks (CT) is the indicator and no account of CC needs to be made since the high level raise is primarily designed to take bidding space away from the opposition. Safety is virtually guaranteed by virtue of the Law of Total Tricks (TNT), but prudence when vulnerable is always wise.

2.2 Limitations of Acol

The beautifully harmonious feeling when you and your partner are communicating together as one with all the subtle nuances and quadraphonic overtones is, I feel, rather like an intimate relationship, one of life's most satisfying experiences. Yet, so many good bridge players seem to settle for mediocrity with their bidding. Is this some sort of fear of intimacy I wonder! Both types of partnerships certainly need optimum communication.

I look at World Championship bidding as the greatest source of learning and see such a challenge because it is with bidding that the ordinary player can really improve and aspire to do things not just as good as the champions but, dare I say, sometimes even better.

In this rather grim world where dreams are too often shattered by harsh political and/or monetary reality it seems that at least with Bridge, a game so often equated with real life, we can afford to follow our dreams of betterment, mainly, but not entirely, unspoilt by 'Government' and other external stressors. As with an intimate relationship, the main requirement is to have a like-minded person who is prepared to go on the shared journey.

The argument regarding which bidding system is best is a most vexed one, probably like all the most intriguing arguments even better for being almost insolvable. The much-vaunted 'Naturalists v Scientists' matches testified to the interest generated in this subject amongst the bridge playing fraternity. For myself, I wonder why it has to be one or the other since both nature and science in balance are sources of great beauty and the challenge surely is to find that balance in bidding. Some side issues in the bridge system argument are indisputable though I believe:

- No bidding system is satisfactory unless you have a very good hand evaluation approach which goes well beyond counting high card points and gets closer to counting realisable tricks.

- No bidding system is satisfactory unless you and your partner thoroughly understand it. The simplicity of the system or ease of learning and retaining should reflect the mutual partnership commitment for hard work and preparation.

- Playing match pointed pairs, a thorough grasp of the peculiar tactics involved is more important than which one of many adequate bidding systems you are using. (I always say on teaching sessions that it is important to realise that the two games, pairs and teams, are as different as say tennis and badminton.) I have also heard it said that the nature of the pairs game is so warped you have to be a little warped yourself to do well at it!

- A player's personality may be important in determining their psychology of bidding, some bidding methods suiting one type of personality more than another. Put simply, it is no good playing with a theoretically ideal bidding system if you do not feel comfortable with it.

However, having said all that, let us not delude ourselves any longer: of course some bidding systems are more effective than others in exactly the same way as some languages are easier to learn and understand than others. The fact that it is difficult to prove objectively, or gain universal agreement does not make it any-the-less true.

I also accept that if we ever came up with a perfect bidding system it would not do a lot for the game since bridge, like life, is fascinating primarily because it always remains a challenge (the effect of utopia is rather like the effect on a dog chasing a car when the car suddenly stops). These are not, I feel however, either realistic or compelling reasons to be satisfied with mediocrity.

Acol, like the English language:

- has been around for a long time
- is a mish mash from various origins
- is no longer pure and unadulterated
- is full of ambiguities and inconsistencies
- is very difficult to learn because of its inherent lack of logic, as it has grown like topsy.

We will explore the analogous effects of time on effectiveness more later, but what are the technical deficiencies of Acol?

Technical Deficiencies of Acol

Weak 1NT

The outstanding weakness of original Acol lies in opening 1NT weak (12-14) when vulnerable, particularly. In pairs, the gains of stopping the opponent's finding their two level suit part score may well offset the occasional big penalty but in teams, even if it only happens every month or so that you really get clobbered, it is very dispiriting to both partnership moral and/or team mate's confidence when you return a minus 500 or 800 to save a part score.

The intriguing thing though is how worshippers of this sacred cow (Acol) reply. It seems that either they accept their bad results philosophically or they tamper with the system choosing to vary the strength of the 1NT opener with vulnerability or devising some fancy gadget to rescue out of 1NT doubled. Trying to make a silk purse out of a sow's ear is not really a solution, I feel, because surely brain-draining clever conventions should ideally be used to combat opponent's effective bidding weapons not your own ineffective or self-destructive ones.

Five Card Majors

This is a case of what Acol does not have that is a deficiency. Ron Klinger, in his book *Five Card Majors*, very tactfully gives eight reasons why 5 card majors are better. Playing a structured system with very competitive obstructive raises of the opened major gives the first hand, 1of a major opener enormous advantage. If 65% of the world's best players prefer some sort of five card major system, then that is probably the nearest we will get to unanimous agreement! I'm convinced – are you?

General

I have frequently suffered the depressing experience in monitoring experienced Acol pairs for Bidding Challenges in Australia and New Zealand. I am amazed, despite longevity of partnership, at what an appalling mess was often made trying to bid some admittedly tricky hands.

There seemed to be several areas leading to mishap that I can recollect:

- Not knowing whether a particular sequence is forcing or not. (I recall hearing jargon like a bid was '95% forcing'. '*What nonsense*' is my tolerant unprejudiced reply.)

- Not knowing whether 4NT is quantitative or Blackwood. (I have known at least two partnerships break-up on this one.)

- Not being sure whether the bidding has guaranteed 5 or only 4 cards in a key suit, or alternatively 4 v 3.

- Not being standardised with your choice of opening bid with 4-4-4-1 type hands or indeed some 4-4-3-2 types.

You can no doubt, if you're honest, think of your own disaster areas.

• • • • •

It seems that Acol was initially devised as a fairly loose bidding system with its drawcard of naturalness and flexibility for those undisciplined souls who liked a fair degree of freedom and opportunity for judgement in their bidding decisions.

Then as the drawcards became drawbacks it has been tampered with so much by so many to try and make it more accurate and effective with the real effect being increased complexity and confusion. The outcome now is that you cannot any longer sit down with a new partner and say we are playing Acol and happily get on with it. You need to say 'whose book?', 'which year?' and 'with what modifications?' unless you do not really mind if you come a cropper sooner and later. Moreover, teaching (and learning) Acol these days is a daymare, or nightmare, because of all the conflicting interpretations.

Having explored most bidding systems I am convinced that Acol would *definitely not* be chosen as the optimum universal bridge language for the 21st century because it is like the English language, fascinating because of its complexity and ambiguity, entrenched because of its historical power basis, although when properly verbalised and understood quite effective and even artistic.

However, unlike a national language, the fact that it has been around for a long time is not a good enough reason to perpetuate a mediocre system in the guise of the standard basic bidding language. For me, Acol has outgrown itself and has lost the right to be the common language because in truth it is no longer either standard or basic. In short, Acol seems to have, rather like one idealistic political party, fallen between two stools as attempts have been made to fine tune it. It has lost its identity and lost its way.

If you still, after my diatribe, have touching faith in Acol I would not like to disturb your tranquillity any longer except to make it clear that my criticism is born of fairly altruistic motives as hopefully you will see in the next section on mindsets (I do not believe in criticising the chairman without being willing to do his job).

Meanwhile, for those who are still wavering try this Acol Bidding test, or use your own favourite other method but without help from the opposition. For once the answers including full sequences will *not* be provided because I have no intention of colluding with, and perpetuating, the Acol myth any longer. Besides I would not really be able to give impressive Acol sequences without cheating more than somewhat. However, optimum final contracts will be suggested in the Appendix followed by the recommended sequences using MIDMAC, the system that we will explore in Section 3.

Bidding Quiz 2

1. ♠ xx
   ♡ AJxx
   ◇ AK9x
   ♣ K10x

   ♠ K9xxx
   ♡ Q10xx
   ◇ x
   ♣ xxx

5. ♠ AQ9x
   ♡ Ax
   ◇ x
   ♣ AJ9xxx

   ♠ 10xxxx
   ♡ Kxxx
   ◇ xxx
   ♣ x

2. ♠ xx
   ♡ Q108x
   ◇ AJx
   ♣ AJxx

   ♠ AJxxx
   ♡ Jx
   ◇ Qxx
   ♣ 10xx

6. ♠ KQ10x
   ♡ A9xx
   ◇ KQ10
   ♣ xx

   ♠ A9x
   ♡ KQ10x
   ◇ xx
   ♣ xxxx

3. ♠ x
   ♡ Qxx
   ◇ AQxxx
   ♣ AJxx

   ♠ A10xx
   ♡ AK10x
   ◇ xx
   ♣ Kxx

7. ♠ K8x
   ♡ AQxx
   ◇ x
   ♣ AJ9xx

   ♠ AQ109
   ♡ xx
   ◇ Axxxxx
   ♣ x

4. ♠ xx
   ♡ K9x
   ◇ KQx
   ♣ AJxxx

   ♠ xx
   ♡ AQ10x
   ◇ Axxx
   ♣ Kxx

8. ♠ Axxx
   ♡ KQJx
   ◇ x
   ♣ J8xx

   ♠ x
   ♡ Axx
   ◇ Axxx
   ♣ xxxxx

9. ♠ x   ♠ AJxxx   11. ♠ –   ♠ KQ1097xx
    ♡ Kxx   ♡ xx   ♡ KQ9xx   ♡ Ax
    ◇ AJxx   ◇ K10xx   ◇ K9x   ◇ Qx
    ♣ KQxxx   ♣ xx   ♣ KJ10xx   ♣ 8x

10. ♠ K   ♠ AJxxx   12. ♠ Jxx   ♠ AQ9x
    ♡ AQ9x   ♡ K8x   ♡ K10   ♡ Axx
    ◇ Jxx   ◇ 10xxx   ◇ AQJxxx   ◇ K10x
    ♣ A10xxx   ♣ x   ♣ Kx   ♣ Axx

2.3 Mindsets and Mindshifts

Please bear with me for a while and examine the strange markings below. What do you see? Take your time before you read on.

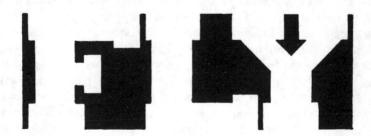

Egyptian writing, perhaps? Well, try again. Maybe this time you are excited because you see the word 'FLY', but unusually depicted in white letters with a black background. We are so used to seeing black writing on a white page, it seems to take a quantum lateral mind shift to transcend the mindset that has become so familiar.

The effect of Acol on the minds of bridge players, particularly in the UK, and no doubt of other long standing bidding languages in other geographical areas is, I believe, an analogous mindset. The excessive inculcation seems to make it difficult to see and accept anything else, which is a pity because that stifles new concepts from being tried and appreciated.

To compound this, the fact that the alerting rules of bridge are based on a particular bidding system rather than some simple principles which define 'natural' bids is evidence of how hidebound, incongruous and distorted our thinking has become. It is almost as if the system, Acol, has become the master and not the slave. How long will it be before the multi 2◊ becomes so popular that we have to alert any 2◊ opening that means something else?!

It is all very well Bridge Managements having a policy of only allowing conventions that are either easy for the opposition to handle or in common usage, but if a new convention is never licensed how does it ever become in common usage?

To penalise a convention because it is too damaging to the opponents seems equally absurd, rather like saying that a tennis player can only play with an old fashioned small 'face' racquet or serve at a maximum speed of 80mph when s/he is playing against a lower seeded opponent. How does the lower grade player ever get better? Perhaps it would make more sense to penalise conventions which are damaging to the proponents rather than the opponents! The analogy with tennis is perhaps apt because both sports are ones that Britain once shone at but now no longer more than occasionally glow a little. If a small country like Iceland can emerge as such a strong force on the international bridge scene, with its own unique brand of bidding, perhaps it is time for Britain to loosen the 'Acol' shackle, let go of the past, learn from it, and look to the future with more prospects of success, particularly in open events. Moreover, unlike tennis we cannot even blame the weather for lack of bridge prowess and progress.

We all have mindsets whether we like it or not. I certainly have more than a few including an aversion to splinter or fragment bids for some reason that totally escapes me other than the obvious observation that they seem unreasonably artificial.

What are the main mindsets that may develop resistance to new bidding concepts that this book is keen to dispel, or, to put it more positively, what mindshifts may be necessary to engage new bidding ideas?

1. Celebrating Progress
I guess if you have stayed the pace this far you must be already dispelling the mindset myth that you cannot bid game or slam, and hope to make it, unless you have more than a certain number of high card points, so you

are already loosening up the boundaries. I trust the excitement you felt when you saw the word FLY for the first time offers sufficient encouragement to offset the fear and trepidation that new unfamiliar concepts inevitably bring with them. In a similar way perhaps the joy of bidding and making a contract that previously seemed out of reach is enough to keep you drinking at the well. A beauty came up last night at our Waddington match which will keep me feeling very 'well' for a while.

North/South Game. Dealer West

```
          ♠ A                     ♠ xxxx
          ♡ K87xxx      N         ♡ Q109x
          ◊ -        W     E      ◊ Kx
          ♣ K9xxxx      S         ♣ AJx
```

West	North	East	South
1♡	1♠	3♡	3♠
4♠	Pass	5♣	Pass
6♡	All Pass		

Nice to freely bid a slam without being pushed when the high card points are evenly split. Incidentally, a small heart to dummy after winning North's ♠K with the ♠A revealed North's heart void. It was not difficult, but very necessary, to play North for the ♣Q, especially, when South tried to cash the ◊A after winning the ♡A.

2. Jump (Mind) Shift

With most approach forcing systems including Acol, a cornerstone is that when you are responding with a good hand (say 16+ points – whatever that means!) you must make a jump shift to immediately establish a game forcing situation. Hence, it may take a while to consider reversing the methodology but look, if you can, at the advantages.

If instead you can make a jump new suit response to show a non forcing limited single suited hand with most of the goodies in that suit, it has the considerable benefit of:

• Making it difficult and dangerous for the opponents to come in.

• Providing a very accurate description in terms of playing trick strength and suit length for opener to act upon.

However, the real bonus of *not* jumping on stronger hands is releasing the use of a slow forcing approach simply by repeating the same suit response at the lowest level so that you can explore the optimum contract with maximum accuracy, naturalness and bidding space.

In Acol after the jump response, opener's rebid is often ambiguous in terms of its strength. It is fine when opener has 17+ points or so, but with a little less the sequence becomes somewhat aimless and distorted. In any case, I thought it was the opponents that were supposed to obstruct our bidding when we are strong, not our partners!

Two examples should hopefully impress this jump 'mind' shift. You are playing Acol:

♠ KJxxx   ♠ x
♡ Kx   ♡ AQJ10xxx
◇ KJx   ◇ 10x
♣ A9x   ♣ Jxx

Now be honest, it is not so easy to get to 3NT is it? Most of the time the bidding would go: 1♠–2♡–2NT–3♡–Pass.

West will explain they have redefined their hand exactly as 15/16 5-3-3-2 or 4-3-3-3 so it is up to East. The bidding is easy with a non forcing jump response showing 8-10 CV and 6-7(p.t.s) because it goes: 1♠–3♡–3NT.

West is in charge and can truly appreciate the value of the K♡ to solidify East's meaty heart suit.

Now let us say East is strong enough to make the traditional jump shift. You are also playing key card Blackwood where the king of the previously bid suit also counts as an ace.

♠ KJxxx   ♠ A
♡ Kx   ♡ AQJ10xxx
◇ KJx   ◇ Ax
♣ A10x   ♣ Jxx

Now be honest, it is not so easy to get to 7♡ because the bidding is likely to go:

West	North	East	South
1♠	Pass	3♡	Pass
3♠	Pass	?	

and the 3♠ is slightly ambiguous to put it mildly. East should still bash in 6♡ though. The slower sequence as proposed would go:

West	North	East	South
1♠	Pass	2♡	Pass
2♠	Pass	3♡	Pass
4♡	Pass	4NT	Pass
5♡	Pass	5NT	Pass
6♡	Pass	7♡	All Pass

East is now in charge and knows that opener (West) has 5+♠, one Ace, three Kings including ♡K, so East can count 13 tricks with any 4-3 division in spades and lots of squeeze chances if spades do not break, all in all well worth bidding the 'grand'. Note that both these hands would be easier to bid if West opening promised 5+ spades, but that is another story!

3 Getting your Mind into Shape

For some reason very obscure to me, bridge players when bidding so-called naturally, rarely think in terms of hand shape. Perhaps it is a case of over indoctrination with HCPs or perhaps it is that Acol and other 'natural' system do not particularly focus on shape of hands.

I know Victor Mollo certainly had a point when he criticised the anti-social and boring aspects of tedious protracted artificial bidding sequences associated with the modern relay methods, which potentially can locate exact shape and even jacks. I know well the feeling 'Wake me up when you have finished, will you?' Maybe it is my poor mathematical inclination or memory that makes these relay ideas rather unappealing to me, because they do depend on memorising by rote codified responses to enquiry bids. Moreover, they are certainly not very forgiving if there is a memory or stress overload lapse by one or both members of the partnership. I think there might have been another reason but I cannot remember!

However, a primary challenge in bidding for me has always been to be able to show hand shape when systematically requested, but naturally. The 35 basic language components provide quite enough combinations and permutations to be linked effectively with hand shape, and an integrated bidding system should be able to do this without boring the socks off the opposition with apparently meaningless verbal or written utterings. As Philip Alder rhetorically asked in a write up for the 1986 World Contract Bridge Championships after 11 rounds of bidding by two very competent relay proponents (Antipodeans Paul Marston and Steven Burgess) to reach 7NT, 'Should one be forced to play with less efficient methods?' I would add 'especially if you can do it with half the bidding space and with a sequence that is essentially natural and intelligible to the logically minded but otherwise uninitiated'. Even allowing for arguments that 'Yes but, common sense is only common to those who have it', I do feel an irresistible urge to try and get your mind into shape!

4 Enquiring Mind

Unless you have played Benjamised Acol with weak two major openings or something else incorporating weak two's, you may not all be familiar with the principle of enquiry bids as the only forcing response to a previous bid. 2NT responses after weak 2♡ and 2♠ are a good case in point. I particularly, and predictably, like the natural rebids which are easy to remember (rebid of the major shows a minimum and any other suit rebid shows a maximum with a useful feature (highcard) in that suit. 3NT rebid by a simple process of elimination also shows a maximum but without a side suit feature, hence a very good major. I became very keen in the late seventies when developing a system called NEAT which had enquiry responses to all opening bids from pass through to 2♠ with *all* other responses very descriptive but non forcing. The essence of the approach was: 'After the enquiry response a subsequent new suit rebid by responder is forcing and *any* subsequent suit bid is game forcing on opener.' Believe me, it works well and opener's rebids are not boring because they are natural within the explicit, or implicit definition of suit length and shape limitations conveyed by the initial opening bid.

5 Undercut

This leads very nicely to a novel, but very exciting concept of undercut bidding.

In the late seventies and early eighties, when I used to be very much involved with contributions to the *New Zealand Bridge Magazine*, when it was edited by the very hard working Lindsay Adams, I had the enjoyable task of reviewing bridge books. One very unusual book was called *First-Up*, the name in fact of an American bidding system presented therein. The underlying principle of the rather evangelically presented system was that regardless of shape your bid as opener or responder was determined by the presence of the lowest denomination, or cheapest biddable suit, which I think was defined as any 4+ suit. This definition had the intriguing consequence, as well as being an obvious and sometimes extreme example of canapé, that if opener or responder on a subsequent rebid chose to bid a lower denomination suit that they had previously bypassed, it naturally promised a good 3 card suit, because they had already denied 4+. This concept facilitated the confident bidding and placement of no trump contracts and was also very appropriate for finding rare Moysian (4-3) fits. As far as I know, the first-up inventors coined the term 'undercut' to describe these specific natural rebids which systematically denied a 4+ suit.

A simple example will give you the idea far better than words:

♠ Jxx		♠ A109x	West	East
♡ AQ10xx		♡ Jx	1♡	1♠
◇ Kxx		◇ Q10	2♡	3♣
♣ Kx		♣ AJ9xx	3◇	3NT

3♣ is not an undercut because it is not a bypassed suit, but 3◇ clearly is because West didn't open 1◇, the correct system bid if 4+◇ (but not 4+♣) were held. On the auction as it went if East does not have honour doubleton in diamonds, or better, the obvious requirement for 3NT bid, then presumably 3♡ or 3♠ or conceivably 4♣ are descriptive alternatives. Note also that this is a more precise version of modern fourth suit forcing ideas.

A slightly more complicated example, involving undercuts by both opener and responder but with a similar satisfactory objective and outcome:

♠ Qxx		♠ AJ10x	West	East
♡ Kx		♡ Qxx	1◇	1♠
◇ AK108x		◇ Jx	2♣	2♡
♣ KJx		♣ A9xx	3NT	

Both 2♣ and 2♡ are clearly undercuts, the latter leading to ideal placement of the inevitable 3NT contract.

• • • • •

So with your new mindshifts at the ready, and appropriately at the half way stage, it is time to put your favourite bidding system to one side, temporarily at least, and focus on a completely new bidding concept MIDMAC, a 'natural' bidding system based on these mindshifts but also incorporating evaluation by tricks from the outset.

From here on in, all hands will have trick value assigned to them, as it changes during the auction in line with developments outlined in Section 3.1. We will use the notation of a number, sometime followed by +(or even ++) or − (or even --) to differentiate between, say, a good 4(4+) or a poor

5(5-) when controls are 1 or 2 better or worse respectively than normal for that CV determined trick value.

You will no doubt recall that if:

- you combine say two 4+ trick hands you will have fair chances to make 9 tricks in combinations.

- you combine, say, two 5- trick hands they should also produce 9 tricks together, as would a 4+ and a 5-.

A hand with a double+ or double- trick value should have its trick value increased or decreased respectively by one in its own right.

'Get it, got it, good!'

Finally, please note that in all shown bidding sequences – all forcing bids will be in **_bold underlined_** type face – all playing trick type bids will be given a designation in playing tricks rather than so many inferred tricks.

3
MIDMAC:
THE BIDDING SYSTEM

Introduction

Every now and again in life you may be really lucky, something happens that seems meant to be, and you think someone is smiling down on you. It happened once in the mid-1970s with a wonderful metallurgical job in New Zealand which came my way when it looked like the job description had not only been written for me, but it could have been written by me. In the mid-1980s a beautiful love/life relationship fell into my path that seemed similarly made-to-measure. Fortuitously, and slightly earlier than on cue for the mid-1990s, '**MIDMAC**' dropped from nowhere into my lap, making so much sense of my earlier bridge bidding meanderings, and in many ways creating much more excitement than the bidding systems that I had previously developed painstakingly from scratch. It's something to do with spontaneity and receptiveness, I expect. Whatever, it's a hard feeling to beat when you realise you are on to something really good.

Like most good inventions it happened by accident and it is essentially so simple. The germ of the essence of MIDMAC, that 1♣ opener would promise one, or both, 4 card majors and 1♢ deny a 4+ major, and therefore by deduction guarantee a 4+ minor quite originally, as far as I know, came from the fertile mind of Sheffielder Terry Jacobs. Having a disorderly junk shop, as Terry does, obviously is good therapy for the brain. Thanks, Terry, for your inspiration. The day you asked me to look over your bidding ideas in that pub on London Road was when it all started.

In the early days the system was called *Big Minor* because the 1♣ and 1♢ openings were so powerful and frequent. Now it is officially called MIDMAC incorporating the essential core ingredient that 1♣ promises a 4 card major and 1♢ promises a 4 card minor hence:

(**Mi**) nor/s = **D** and (**Ma**) jor/s = **C**. Get it?

Another suggested name, *Big Mac* failed through lack of sponsorship!

With the primary aim of producing a simple natural constructive system but which incorporated the mind shifts described in Section 2.3, MIDMAC very quickly developed within the framework that all bids are uniquely defined in terms of tricks, and the level of bid at any stage of the auction is set by the minimum combined tricks.

Building up from the basic meaning of 1♣ and 1◊ and grafting on the advantages of essentially natural 5+ card one of a major and 6+ card two of a minor opening bids so valuable for obstructive fit bidding, including T.N.T., the system magically fell into place with a minimum of fuss and need for early change. 1NT took over the role of the big catch-all opener, not by default but by desire.

I recall the euphoria in those early heady weeks of 1991 as I raced through thousands of hands expecting, but not finding, significant flaws. Instead the realisation was that MIDMAC could not only easily bid optimum contracts, but also could stay out of unmakeable ones that other systems could not. Being somewhat perfectionistic by nature, I became my own devil's advocate and somewhat masochistically tried to find, with the help of friends and partners, hands that could beat the system. I finally had to admit defeat because using the hand valuation methods described so far it seems difficult to construct a hand that MIDMAC struggles with. So that is quite a challenging statement for those hard-nosed readers who do not believe in miracles. What more can I say?

3.1 MIDMAC The System Structure

The main opening suit bids 1♣ –> 2◊ are all constructive bids which promise a minimum number (4) and a maximum number (7) of tricks (CV range 11-19). The 1NT opener, the strong constructive bid, takes over with 8+ tricks (or good 7) and CV of typically 20+.

There are also a range of supplementary opening bids 2♡ –> 3NT which are primarily obstructive (defensive, pre-emptive but nevertheless very descriptive) which deny more that a certain number of controls but promise a certain number of playing tricks, typical of long single suited hands or marked two suiters.

Moreover, specific responses to all main opening bids are available to cover descriptive playing trick type hands when they happen to be in 3rd or 4th position rather than 1st or 2nd.

In all future sequences in this book these descriptive obstructive playing trick type openers and responses will be shown by defining in terms of p.t.s. whilst all forcing bids will be shown in **bold and underlined**.

Frequently within the MIDMAC bidding system we refer to a **good** suit. This may need definition as follows:

Suit Length	Honours	(A K or Q)
2/3	1+	
4	2+	
5	3+ or 2 of top 3 but inc. 10 or jack	
6	2 of top 3	

So much for definitions, now for the real stuff:

Main Opening Bids (Constructive)

Bid	Tricks	CV	Description
Pass	0-3	0-10	any shape
1♣	4-6	11-19	all 4 major/s hands – any shape
1◇	4-6	11-19	not 4 + major or 6 + minor – any shape
1♡/1♠	4-6/7	11-19	5 + major, could have longer minor
<u>1NT</u>	good 7+	20+	includes 8/9 (p.t.) hands any shape
2♣/2◇	4-6/7	11-19	6 + minor not 4 + major

Supplementary Opening Bids (Obstructive)

Bid	Playing tricks	CV	Description
2♡/2♠	4-6	6-10	6 major or good 5 with 4 + minor
2NT->3♡	5-7	6-10	transfer pre-empt showing next suit up
3♠	7	11-13	*any* solid 7 card suit, nothing outside
3NT	7-8	11-16	*any* solid 7 card suit, something outside

If opponents, curse them, interfere over our opening bids we play ongoing doubles, or redoubles but only after 1♣ and 1◇ openers. Doubles or redoubles after intervention of opening bids 1♡ –> 3NT are very much penalty oriented.

As far as possible, for simplicity and ease on memory, responders' and openers' reaction to intervention remains little changed from normal constructive bidding.

The main opening bids provide the life blood of MIDMAC. You may have already noted that the usual weak, intermediate or strong no trump openings are incorporated within 1♣ or 1◇ depending on whether you do, or do not, have a 4 card major respectively.

The nominated supplementary opening bids have been arranged to provide a balance to the complete bidding approach in conjunction with modern bidding ideas. Some of these may seem alarmingly novel, so you may have alternative preferences for these obstructive bids which you can use without substantially upsetting the integrity of MIDMAC.

An intriguing feature of MIDMAC is that lower ranking opening bids occur more frequently and higher bids less frequently in an almost perfect frequency distribution pattern.

Percentage probability of each opening bid based on analysis of 1000 world championship hands (1992 Olympiad).

Midmac Opening Bid	Pass	1♣	1◇	1♡	1♠	1NT	2♣	2◇	2♡	2♠	→
% (nearest whole no)	47*	16	9	8	8	5	2	2	1	1	1

*Note % pass is lower than most bidding systems thus limiting strength of re-opening bids for passed hands.

Now let us look at each main opening bid in turn:

3.2 Main Opening Bids

OPENING BID ONE CLUB

• 4-6 tricks – all hands with 4 major/s regardless of shape. Club length can be as short as zero because 1♣ opener can include a long minor or be 3 suited, as well as balanced.

Main Responses

Response	Tricks	CV	Description
Pass	<2	0-5	typically club tolerance
1◇	>2	>6	forcing artificial enquiry
1♡/1♠	>2	>6	good 4+ major
1NT	2-3	6-9	balanced, denies 4+ major
2 suit	4-5p.t.	6-10	good 5+ suit
2NT	>5	>13	4+ both majors, 4+ controls
3 suit	5-6p.t.	8-10	good 6+ suit
3NT	5	13-15	balanced, denies 4 + major

If opponents interfere over 1♣, up to and including 3♠, double or redouble replaces the 1◇ enquiry response as the only force, although 2NT retains its original meaning. All other non forcing responses are unaffected in their meaning by intervention. Notice also that the pass by responder of 1♣(Dble) infers a club suit.

Further Bidding:

Rebid	Tricks	CV	Description
1♣, <u>1◇</u>: 1♡	4-5	11-16	4♡ not 4♠
1♠	4-5	11-16	4♠ not 4♡
1NT	4-5	11-15	4♡ & 4♠ Balanced
2♣/2◇	4-5	11-16	4♡ & 4♠ & 4/5 bid minor
2♡–>3◇	6	17-19	as for 1♡ –> 2◇ except 2NT 16-17
3NT	6+	18-19	as for 1NT & 2NT

If 1◇ responder now rebids a new non jump suit, including diamonds, a rebid of this suit is forcing thereafter on opener to game. If opener showed a minimum (4-5 tricks) on first rebid they are expected to clarify by minimum or jump bid at the next opportunity.

Rebid	Tricks	CV	Description
1♣, <u>1♡</u>: 1♠	4-5	11-16	4♠ 4-1-4-4 or 4-0-5-4
1NT	4-5	11-15	4♠ balanced
2♣/2◇	4-5	11-16	4♠ 5+ minor
2♡	4-5	11-16	good 3 or 4♡ + shortage
2♠–>3♡	6	17-19	as for 1♠–>2♡ except 2NT 16-17
3NT	6+	18-19	as for 1NT & 2NT
3♠ 4♣ 4◇	7+	20-22	4♡ natural unbalanced
4♡	7+	20-22	4♡ natural fairly balanced

If 1♡ responder now rebids hearts at the lowest level (non jump) this is forcing on opener thereafter to game. Opener clarifies strength within 4-5 trick rebid range by minimum or jump bid at the next opportunity.

Rebid	Tricks	CV	Description
1♣, <u>1♠</u>: 1NT	4-5	11-15	4♡ balanced or 1-4-4-4 (min)
2♣/2◇	4-5	11-16	4♡ 5+ minor
2♡	5	14-16	4♡ 4/4 or 4/5 minors
2♠	4-5	11-16	good 3 or 4♠ + shortage
2NT–>3♠	6	17-19	as for 1NT–>2♠ except 2NT 16-17
3NT	6+	18-19	as for 1NT & 2NT
4♣ 4◇ 4♡	7+	20-22	4♠ otherwise natural unbalanced
4♠	7+	20-22	4♠ fairly balanced

If 1♠ responder now rebids spades at the lowest level (non jump) this is forcing on opener thereafter to game. Opener clarifies strength within 4-5 trick range by minimum or jump rebid at the next opportunity.

1♣, 1NT:	Pass	4-5	11-15	Balanced
	2♣/2◇	4-5	11-16	5+ minor unspecified 4 major/s
	2♡	5	14-16	4♡ and 4/4 or 4/5 minors
	2♠	5	14-16	4♠ and 4/4 or 4/5 minors
	2NT	5+	16-17	Balanced
	3♣->3♠	6	17-19	as for 2♣->2♠
	3NT	6+	18-19	Balanced

Now after that gruelling indoctrination try bidding the hands in Quizzes 3 and 4 all incorporating the 1♣ opener. Answers are in Appendix 1. Quiz 3 is intended to be more straightforward than Quiz 4.

Bidding Quiz 3
1♣ Openers MIDMAC

1. ♠ AK8x   ♠ J9x   5. ♠ AJ9x   ♠ 10x
    ♡ xx   ♡ Axxx   ♡ AJxx   ♡ Q9x
    ◇ xx   ◇ Qxxx   ◇ K9x   ◇ A108x
    ♣ AQxxx   ♣ xx   ♣ Qx   ♣ KJxx

2. ♠ AK8x   ♠ J109x   6. ♠ KJxx   ♠ xx
    ♡ xx   ♡ Axx   ♡ 9x   ♡ AJ108xx
    ◇ xx   ◇ Kxxx   ◇ J98x   ◇ Axx
    ♣ AQxxx   ♣ Kx   ♣ AQJ   ♣ xx

3. ♠ Kxx   ♠ AQ9x   7. ♠ A9xx   ♠ x
    ♡ Axxx   ♡ xx   ♡ x   ♡ AJ9xx
    ◇ x   ◇ J9xxx   ◇ K9x   ◇ J8xx
    ♣ KQxxx   ♣ xx   ♣ AQ10xx   ♣ K8x

4. ♠ K108x   ♠ AJ9x   8. ♠ AK   ♠ QJ108x
    ♡ Axxx   ♡ x   ♡ A10xx   ♡ xx
    ◇ -   ◇ J9xxx   ◇ Qx   ◇ Kxxx
    ♣ AKxxx   ♣ xxx   ♣ Q109xx   ♣ xx

9. ♠ Ax   ♠ KQJ10x
    ♡ A10xx   ♡ xx
    ◊ Ax   ◊ Qxxx
    ♣ Q109xx   ♣ xx

11. ♠ Axxx   ♠ x
    ♡ x   ♡ AQxxx
    ◊ KJ9x   ◊ Qxx
    ♣ K109x   ♣ Jxxx

10. ♠ AJx   ♠ 9xx
    ♡ AQxx   ♡ x
    ◊ Kxx   ◊ Jxx
    ♣ Kxx   ♣ AQ109xx

12. ♠ x   ♠ Axxxx
    ♡ AQxx   ♡ J9x
    ◊ KQxx   ◊ xx
    ♣ AK10x   ♣ Qxx

Bidding Quiz 4 – 1♣ Openers MIDMAC

1. ♠ A109x   ♠ J
    ♡ AK10x   ♡ 98x
    ◊ 10x   ◊ AK97
    ♣ KJx   ♣ Q8xxx

7. ♠ AJxx   ♠ Kx
    ♡ x   ♡ A10xx
    ◊ KQJ9xxx   ◊ 10x
    ♣ x   ♣ A109xx

2. ♠ A8xx   ♠ KQ10x
    ♡ x   ♡ Axx
    ◊ KJx   ◊ A9xx
    ♣ AKJxx   ♣ Qx

8. ♠ KQxx   ♠ 10x
    ♡ AJxx   ♡ 9x
    ◊ K10xxx   ◊ A9xx
    ♣ –   ♣ AKJ9x

3. ♠ KQJ10   ♠ 9x
    ♡ Qx   ♡ AK9xx
    ◊ A10xxx   ◊ Q98xx
    ♣ Qx   ♣ A

9. ♠ AJ9x   ♠ x
    ♡ xxx   ♡ KQ109xxx
    ◊ Ax   ◊ Kxx
    ♣ KQxx   ♣ Ax

4. ♠ KQ10x   ♠ 9x
    ♡ x   ♡ AQ108
    ◊ A109xx   ◊ Qxx
    ♣ QJx   ♣ K9xx

10. ♠ xx   ♠ AQ109xx
    ♡ K10xx   ♡ Qxx
    ◊ AQ10x   ◊ Jx
    ♣ KQ9   ♣ Jx

5. ♠ AK8x   ♠ QJ109xx
    ♡ AQxx   ♡ 10x
    ◊ –   ◊ QJxx
    ♣ A109xx   ♣ x

11. ♠ Qxx   ♠ AJ9
    ♡ AKJx   ♡ Q9xx
    ◊ Qx   ◊ AKxx
    ♣ AQ97   ♣ xx

6. ♠ Q1097   ♠ Axx
    ♡ AJxx   ♡ KQxx
    ◊ A9   ◊ Jxx
    ♣ xxx   ♣ 10xx

12. ♠ AQ9x   ♠ Jxx
    ♡ K7x   ♡ AJ986
    ◊ AK9   ◊ 10x
    ♣ Jxx   ♣ K10x

13. ♠ AKJx   ♠ Qx
    ♡ A10x   ♡ KQ9x
    ◇ xx   ◇ J10xxx
    ♣ xxxx   ♣ xx

14. ♠ AKJx   ♠ Qx
    ♡ AQ9   ♡ K10xx
    ◇ xx   ◇ J10xxx
    ♣ xxxx   ♣ xx

15. ♠ AJxx   ♠ 10xx
    ♡ Jx   ♡ KQxx
    ◇ A10x   ◇ QJ9xx
    ♣ Qxxx   ♣ x

16. ♠ AJxx   ♠ Q9x
    ♡ Jxx   ♡ Kxxx
    ◇ Ax   ◇ QJ9xx
    ♣ Qxxx   ♣ x

17. ♠ Axxx   ♠ J9
    ♡ Qxx   ♡ Kxxx
    ◇ x   ◇ QJ9xx
    ♣ AQJ9x   ♣ xx

18. ♠ Axxx   ♠ Q9
    ♡ AJ9   ♡ K10xx
    ◇ x   ◇ QJ9xx
    ♣ K9xxx   ♣ xx

19. ♠ AJxx   ♠ x
    ♡ xxx   ♡ KQ10x
    ◇ AQ10x   ◇ J9xx
    ♣ Qx   ♣ J10xx

20. ♠ AJxx   ♠ x
    ♡ Jx   ♡ KQ10x
    ◇ A10x   ◇ 98xx
    ♣ Q9xx   ♣ K10xx

21. ♠ AJ108   ♠ Qx
    ♡ AQx   ♡ xxx
    ◇ 10xxx   ◇ KQ9x
    ♣ Jx   ♣ AQ109

22. ♠ AQJ8   ♠ 10x
    ♡ Axx   ♡ Qxx
    ◇ 10xxx   ◇ KQxx
    ♣ Jx   ♣ AQ109

23. ♠ Jxx   ♠ Q9x
    ♡ AQJ8   ♡ 10x
    ◇ Axxx   ◇ KJxx
    ♣ Jx   ♣ AQ109

24. ♠ Axxx   ♠ xx
    ♡ AQ   ♡ KJxxx
    ◇ Kxxx   ◇ QJx
    ♣ xxx   ♣ xxx

OPENING BID ONE DIAMOND

CV 11-19 tricks 4-6 - denies 4+ major or 6+ minor, balanced or minor 2 suiter. Note that 1◇ automatically promises at least a doubleton in both minors.

Main Responses

Response	Tricks	CV	Description
Pass	<2	0-5	
1♡/1♠	>2	>6	good 4+ major
1NT	2-3	6-9	balanced

2♣/2◇	>3	>10	4+ suit
2♡/2♠	4/5p.t.	6-10	good 5+ major - not forcing
2NT	>5	>13	both minors 4+ controls
3 suit	5/6p.t.	8-10	good 6+ suit not forcing
3NT	5	13-15	balanced can include 4 major/s
4♣	5		pre-emptive minor two suiter

If opponents interfere over 1◇ up to and including 3♠, x or xx becomes ongoing showing balance of power. All other responses retain their original meaning but are not forcing except 2NT of course. Notice that pass by responder after 1◇(Dble) infers a reasonable diamond holding.

Further Bidding

	Rebid	Tricks	CV	Description
1◇, **1♡**:	1♠	4-5	11-16	3 good ♠, short ♡ both minors
	1NT	4-5	11-15	balanced
	2♣/2◇	4-5	11-16	5 specified minor 4/5 other minor, not 3 good ♡ or ♠
	2♡	4-5	11-16	3 good ♡ + shortage for ruffing
	2♠->3♡	6	17-19	as for 1♠ –> 2♡ except 2NT is 16-17
	3NT	6+	18-19	balanced as for 1NT & 2NT
	3♠ 4♣ 4◇	7+	20-22	3 good ♡ natural unbalanced
	4♡	7+	20-22	3 good ♡ fairly balanced great controls therefore both 4 minors 2-3-4-4

	Rebid	Tricks	CV	Description
1◇ **1♠**:	1NT	4-5	11-15	balanced – denies 3 good ♠ if shortage
	2♣/2◇	4-5	11-16	5 specified minor 4/5 in other minor
	2♡	5	14-16	3 good ♡ not 3 good ♠ both minors
	2♠	4-5	11-16	3 good ♠ + shortage for ruffing
	2NT->3♠	6	17-19	as for 1NT–> 2♠ except 2NT 16-17
	3NT	6+	18-19	balanced as for 1NT and 2NT
	4♣ 4◇ 4♡	7+	20-22	3 good ♠ natural unbalanced
	4♠	7+	20-22	3 good ♠ fairly balanced ... both minors 3-2-4-4

1◇, 1NT: Pass	4-5	11-15	balanced
2♣/2◇	4-5	11-16	5 specified minor 4/5 other minor
2♡	5	14-16	3 good hearts 1-3-4-5 or 0-3-5-5
2♠	5	14-16	3 good spades 3-1-4-5 or 3-0-5-5
2NT	5+	16-17	balanced
3♣–>3♠	6	17-19	as for 2♣ –> 2♠
3NT	6+	18-19	balanced.

1◇, 2♣: 2◇	4	11-13	5 diamonds balanced ... 3-3-5-2 type
2♡/2♠	4	11-13	good 3 major, other major poor doubleton or tripleton
2NT	4	11-13	stop or partial stop both majors balanced
3♣	5	14-16	4/5♣ not flat i.e. not 3334
3◇–>3NT	5	14-16	as for 2◇–>2NT but 1 trick more
4♣	6	17-19	4/5♣ unbalanced
4◇ 4♡ 4♠	7+	20-22	4/5♣ otherwise natural unbalanced
4NT	6+	17-19	Balanced but useful honour in clubs.
5♣	7	20-22	4/5♣ but fairly balanced 2-2-4-5 type

1◇, 2◇: as for 1◇, 2♣:

Now after all that tedium try bidding the hands in quizzes 5 and 6. Once again you should find the second set harder than the first. Answers are in Appendix 1.

Bidding Quiz 5
MIDMAC 1◇ Opening

1. ♠ xx   ♠ KQ10x   3. ♠ x   ♠ AQ109xx
    ♡ 10x   ♡ AJ9x   ♡ Axx   ♡ xx
    ◇ AKQx   ◇ xxx   ◇ KQxxx   ◇ xx
    ♣ AKJxx   ♣ 9x   ♣ Kxxx   ♣ Jxx

2. ♠ Kxx   ♠ Qx   4. ♠ J9x   ♠ AQxxx
    ♡ x   ♡ AKQxx   ♡ A10x   ♡ xxx
    ◇ AJ9xx   ◇ xxx   ◇ Ax   ◇ Q10x
    ♣ A108x   ♣ KJx   ♣ AQxxx   ♣ Kx

5. ♠ Kxx   ♠ AQ9xx   9. ♠ Ax   ♠ xxx
    ♡ KJx   ♡ 10xx   ♡ x   ♡ AQ9xx
    ◇ K9x   ◇ Q10x   ◇ AQ10xx   ◇ J8xx
    ♣ AJxx   ♣ Qx   ♣ AKxxx   ♣ x

6. ♠ K8x   ♠ A10xx   10. ♠ xx   ♠ AQx
    ♡ x   ♡ Axxxx   ♡ Ax   ♡ Q109xx
    ◇ KJxx   ◇ xx   ◇ AKQxx   ◇ xxx
    ♣ A10xxx   ♣ xx   ♣ K10xx   ♣ Jx

7. ♠ AJx   ♠ Qx   11. ♠ x   ♠ AQ108x
    ♡ Qx   ♡ A10xxx   ♡ K10   ♡ Qxx
    ◇ AJx   ◇ 9xx   ◇ KJ9xx   ◇ A10x
    ♣ QJ9xx   ♣ Kxx   ♣ AQ9xx   ♣ Jx

8. ♠ J9x   ♠ AK8x   12. ♠ AKx   ♠ QJ108
    ♡ A10x   ♡ xxxx   ♡ x   ♡ Axxxx
    ◇ Ax   ◇ Q10x   ◇ AJxx   ◇ Kx
    ♣ AQxxx   ♣ xx   ♣ KQ10xx   ♣ Ax

Bidding Quiz 6.
MIDMAC 1◇ Opening

1. ♠ x   ♠ A108xx   4. ♠ AKJ   ♠ xx
    ♡ KQx   ♡ AJ9x   ♡ x   ♡ Axx
    ◇ KQxx   ◇ xx   ◇ AKJx   ◇ Qx
    ♣ AQ10xx   ♣ 9x   ♣ Kxxxx   ♣ AQ10xxx

2. ♠ KQ10   ♠ xx   5. ♠ Kxx   ♠ xx
    ♡ 10xx   ♡ AJxx   ♡ AJ9   ♡ 8x
    ◇ Axx   ◇ KQJxxx   ◇ QJ108x   ◇ AK9xxx
    ♣ KQ10x   ♣ x   ♣ A10   ♣ Jxx

3. ♠ AJx   ♠ xx   6. ♠ xx   ♠ AQ10
    ♡ KJx   ♡ Ax   ♡ AQJ   ♡ xx
    ◇ AKxxx   ◇ xx   ◇ xxx   ◇ QJ9xx
    ♣ xx   ♣ AKQxxxx   ♣ AKQxx   ♣ xxx

7.	♠ AQ10	♠ x	10.	♠ xx	♠ Jx
	♡ xxx	♡ Kx		♡ Axx	♡ x
	◇ Kx	◇ Q109xxx		◇ QJ9x	◇ A108xx
	♣ A10xxx	♣ KJxx		♣ KQxx	♣ J108xx
8.	♠ AKx	♠ Qx	11.	♠ xx	♠ A10xxx
	♡ -	♡ AKQ10x		♡ A108	♡ QJ9x
	◇ Q10xxx	◇ J9x		◇ A8xx	◇ Kx
	♣ KJ9xx	♣ Qxx		♣ AKxx	♣ xx
9.	♠ AK10	♠ Jx	12.	♠ x	♠ Axxxx
	♡ xx	♡ A109xx		♡ AJx	♡ K1098
	◇ AQ109x	◇ xx		◇ KJ9x	◇ Axx
	♣ Jxx	♣ AKxx		♣ AQ9xx	♣ x

Approximately half all MIDMAC hands that are opened with a positive bid involve a 1♣ or 1◇ opening and because they are temptingly easy to overcall it is important that you practise coping with intervention – not just intervention immediately after the 1♣ or 1◇ opener, but also intervention after the response to these openings.

Let us say the 1♣ or 1◇ opener made by West has been overcalled by North and an ongoing double (or redouble) made by East. Opener's rebids are entirely natural and generally unaffected by intervention but including the penalty pass. The only possible ambiguity, he says optimistically, is when the opening is 1♣ and the overcall was 1 major or 2 major. Now after East's double 1NT/2NT or 2 minor/3 minor by opener may not necessarily show both majors but could be a hand with 4 card major holdings in opponent's suit but not willing to make a penalty pass. If as opener you do have the major other than the one opponents have shown then it should always be bid naturally to be clear. This principle also applies after a 1◇ opener if you have a good 3 card major and ruffing values in the opponent's major.

Continuing the approach after West has opened 1♣ or 1◇ but now South (opener's RHO) interferes after East's response, doubles by West or East are primarily for penalties. However, if North and/or South bid up to 3♠ without a response from East, West's reopening double is primarily takeout.

• • • • •

OPENING BIDS ONE HEART/ONE SPADE

CV 11-19 tricks 4-6/7 all hands with 5+ major, so a longer minor is a rare possibility. (Note double or redouble of intervention is penalties.)

Main Responses

Bid	Tricks	CV	Description
Pass	<2	0-5	
1♡, **1♠**:	>2	>6	4+ spades any shape
1NT	2-3	6-9	Balanced or misfit
2♣/2◇	>3	>10	4+ minor any shape
1♠, 2♡	>3	>10	5+ hearts any shape
2 Raise	2-3	6-10	3+ good major + shortage for ruffing
1♡,2♠	4(p.t.)	6-10	good 5+ ♠
2NT	>5	>13	4+ opened major 4+ controls
3 New suit	5/6(p.t.)	8-10	one-suiter 6+ most values in suit
3 Raise	4	11-13	4+ opened major unbalanced
3NT	5	13-15	Balanced
4 Raise	5	14-16	4 opened major unbalanced

In his book *Five Card Majors*, Ron Klinger makes the virtues of 5 card majors quite clear so I will not extol them further here.

After all the forcing responses opener simply rebids naturally:

- at the 2 level with min 4 tricks
- at the 3 level with   5 tricks
- at the 4 level with   6+ tricks (which of course infers tolerance for responder's suit)

Remember too if opener has a longer minor s/he just keeps rebidding it.

After the limit responses opener is well placed to pass or otherwise suggest the final contract which responder can treat as invitational if not already at game level.

This time the Quiz (7) takes a slightly different format.

- The first part asks you to try and work out the meaning (shape and tricks) of all opener's rebids 2◇ –> 5♣ after a sequence 1♠, 2♣: based on the guidelines provided by:

1.   The bidding developments already given for 1◇, 2♣/2◇.

2.   The general MIDMAC principle that you bid or rebid naturally to the level denoted by minimum number of combined tricks.

*   The second part gives you twelve hands to top up your understanding of a variety of sequences starting with the 1 ♡ or 1 ♠ opener.

Answers are in the Appendix.

Bidding Quiz 7
Part II MIDMAC 1 Major Openings

1.	♠ KJ97xx	♠ Q8x	7.	♠ Ax	♠ 10x
	♡ AKx	♡ Q		♡ AKQJx	♡ 10x
	◇ Jx	◇ AKxxxx		◇ Q	◇ AKxxxx
	♣ Jx	♣ AQx		♣ QJ10xx	♣ 9xx

2.	♠ K10x	♠ Qxx	8.	♠ AKQJxx	♠ 9x
	♡ AQ9xx	♡ J10		♡ Q9	♡ AJ10
	◇ K10xx	◇ A9xx		◇ 10xx	◇ 9xxx
	♣ A	♣ Kxxx		♣ Qx	♣ A8xx

3.	♠ Qx	♠ KJ9xx	9.	♠ -	♠ KJ1087x
	♡ KQ10xx	♡ xx		♡ AJ9xx	♡ xx
	◇ AJx	◇ K10x		◇ 9x	◇ Qxx
	♣ KJ8	♣ Q10x		♣ KQ87xx	♣ xx

4.	♠ J1087x	♠ AQ	10.	♠ KJxxx	♠ 9x
	♡ x	♡ Axxx		♡ Q	♡ Jxxxxx
	◇ AQxx	◇ xx		◇ AK97	◇ x
	♣ KQx	♣ J10xxx		♣ AQx	♣ K10xx

5.	♠ A	♠ xxxx	11.	♠ AQJ9xx	♠ 10xx
	♡ KJ108x	♡ Qxx		♡ K	♡ QJ109x
	◇ K9xxx	◇ Axxx		◇ A107x	◇ x
	♣ xx	♣ KJ		♣ Qx	♣ A9xx

6.	♠ AQ109x	♠ Kx	12.	♠ AQJ10xxx	♠ K9x
	♡ x	♡ Jxx		♡ AQ97	♡ Kxx
	◇ AKJx	◇ Qxx		◇ J	◇ Axxx
	♣ xxx	♣ AQ109x		♣ 9	♣ Jxx

OPENING BIDS TWO CLUBS AND TWO DIAMONDS

CV 11-19 Tricks 4-7 6+ Minor no 4+ major (note double or redouble of intervention is penalties).

Main Responses to 2♣ Opener

Response	Tricks	CV	Description
Pass	0-2	0-7	
2◊	>3	>8	artificial forcing enquiry
2♡/2♠	4/5(p.t.)	6-10	good 5+ suit
2NT	4	11-12	balanced or misfit
3♣	4	11-13	good 3 + ♣ unbalanced
3◊/3♡/3♠	5/6(p.t.)	8-10	good 6+ suit
3NT	5	13-15	balanced
4♣	5	14-16	4+♣ unbalanced
5♣	6	17-19	4+♣ unbalanced
4NT	7+	20+	4+♣ genuine raise to 5♣ 5 + controls

Further Bidding

Rebid	Tricks	CV	Description
2♣, 2◊ : 2♡/2♠	4-5	11-16	good 3+ suit
2NT	4-5	11-16	fairly balanced or 3 + ◊
3♣	4-5	11-16	7 + ♣
3◊	6-7	17-19	4 + ◊
3♡/3♠	6-7	17-19	good 3+ suit
3NT	6-7	17-19	fairly balanced
4♣	7	17-19	unbalanced 1 loser 7+ ♣

A new suit by the 2◊ responder is now natural and game forcing.

Note that opener in rebidding after 2◊ response denies holdings for lower available bids within specified point range.

Main Responses to 2◊ Opener.

Response	Tricks	CV	Description
Pass	0-2	0-7	
2♡	>3	>8	artificial forcing enquiry
2♠	4/5(p.t.)	6-10	good 5+ suit
2NT	4	11-12	balanced or misfit
3♣/3♡/3♠	5/6(p.t.)	8-10	good 6+ suit
3◊	4	11-13	good 3+◊ unbalanced
3NT	5	13-15	balanced
4◊	5	14-16	4+◊ unbalanced

5◊	6	17-19	4+◊ unbalanced
4NT	7+	20+	4+◊ genuine raise to 5◊
			5+ controls

Further Bidding

Rebid		Tricks	CV	Description
2◊,**2♡**	2♠	4-5	11-16	Good 3♠
	2NT	4-5	11-16	fairly balanced or 3 good ♡
	3♣	4-5	11-16	4+♣
	3◊	4-5	11-16	7+◊
	3♡/3♠	6-7	17-19	Good 3 major
	3NT	6-7	17-19	fairly balanced or 3+ clubs
	4◊	7	17-19	1 loser 7 + ◊ suit unbalanced

A new suit by the 2♡ responder is now game forcing.

The consequent clarity of bidding provided by opening 5+ card majors is continued with the 6+ minor openings which are streamlined by not having a 4+ major included therein, hence it is often possible to show shape exactly but naturally.

Try bidding Quiz 8 to get used to these 2 minor openings. I do not think it will take you long. Answers in Appendix 1.

Bidding Quiz 8
MIDMAC 2♣ & 2◊ openers.

1. ♠ -   ♠ Q10xxx   4. ♠ –   ♠ K109xx
    ♡ Axx   ♡ xx   ♡ xxx   ♡ AK10xx
    ◊ K109x   ◊ AQxx   ◊ AQ10x   ◊ xx
    ♣ AQ9xxx   ♣ Jx   ♣ AKQxxx   ♣ x

2. ♠ Qx   ♠ Axxx   5. ♠ 108x   ♠ x
    ♡ Kx   ♡ Jxx   ♡ AKx   ♡ J9x
    ◊ Jx   ◊ Qxxx   ◊ KJ9xxx   ◊ Ax
    ♣ AKQ10xxx   ♣ xx   ♣ x   ♣ AKQ108xx

3. ♠ AKx   ♠ xx   6. ♠ Kxx   ♠ AQ10x
    ♡ J9x   ♡ AK1087x   ♡ x   ♡ Ax
    ◊ x   ◊ xxx   ◊ AQJ10xx   ◊ Kx
    ♣ AQ10xxx   ♣ xx   ♣ Qxx   ♣ AJxxx

7. ♠ Axx	♠ 10x	10. ♠ Ax	♠ 8x
♡ x	♡ KJ108xx	♡ 9x	♡ K10
◊ Qxx	◊ K10xxx	◊ xx	◊ A109xx
♣ KQ97xx	♣ −	♣ AQJ1098x	♣ Kxxx
8. ♠ J8x	♠ AQ107	11. ♠ xx	♠ Kxx
♡ −	♡ AJ87x	♡ KQx	♡ xx
◊ AKJ8xx	◊ Q10xx	◊ AQ10xxx	◊ x
♣ K109x	♣ −	♣ Ax	♣ KQJ8xxx
9. ♠ AQx	♠ 10x	12. ♠ A8x	♠ KQJ9xx
♡ 10xx	♡ KJ8	♡ Axx	♡ x
◊ x	◊ AJ10xxx	◊ x	◊ Axxx
♣ AJ10xxx	♣ Kx	♣ AQxxxx	♣ Kx

So buzzing with euphoria, I trust, after those exhilarating and beautiful sequences starting with the dynamic two minor openings are you ready for the really unusual no trump, the one that opponents will not double for penalties? So give a Viennese re-welcome to 1NT Big and Beautiful, and the last (but most) of the main opening MIDMAC bids.

OPENING BID 1NT

All hands with CV of 20+ any shape but also including 8/9 p.t. hands providing 5 + HCP controls.

(Double or redouble of intervention is primarily penalties.)

1NT, the opening bid, that brings music to the ears and blood to the head.

Main Responses

Response	Tricks	CV	Description
Pass			**no** you don't!
2♣	0-2	0-7	any shape but excludes semi positives 3◊ –> 3NT
2◊/2♡/2♠	>3	>8	natural positive
2NT	>3	>8	balanced positive
3♣	>3	>8	natural good 5+ suit positive
3◊/3♡/3♠/3NT	4/5 (p.t.)	5-7	6 or 7 card suit, most HCP in long suit, 3NT = club suit

All positive responses to 1NT are game forcing.

Further Bidding

	Rebid	Tricks	CV	Description
1NT, **2♣**:	**2◇**	>8	>22	22+ balanced or gameforce unbalanced
	2♡/2♠	7/8 (p.t.)	20-22	natural nonforcing
	2NT	7	20-21	balanced
	3♣/3◇	8 (p.t.)	20-22	natural non forcing
	3♡/3♠	9 (p.t.)	20-22	natural 7+ solid suit non forcing
	3NT	9 (p.t.)	20-22	long solid 7 suit - stops or partial stops in other suits slightly gambling

	Rebid	Tricks	CV	Description
1NT, **2♣: 2◇**,	**2♡/2♠**	2	5-7	4 or poor 5 suit
	2NT	0-1	0-4	double negative any shape (unlikely to produce makeable 3NT opposite opener's 22-23 balanced hand, the only non absolutely game forcing holding possible.)
	3♣/3◇	2	5-7	good 5 or poor 6 suit
	3♡/3♠	2	5-7	good 5 or poor 6 suit
	3NT	2	5-7	balanced but not 4 major or good 5 minor

Note that once 1NT opener has rebid 2◇ all rebids by responder other than 2NT are game forcing.

After all 2NT rebids by opener and 2NT response or rebid by responder, 3♣ is Baron style asking for suits to be bid in ascending order.

After 2NT rebid by 1NT opener following responder's 2♣ negative, 3♣ is Staymanic and 3◇, 3♡ transfers to hearts and spades respectively.

By the way, after responder to 1NT has made the negative 2♣ response and opener subsequently makes a key card ask, responder is allowed to show the K of the previously bid suit without another A since opener knows s/he cannot have an A and a K otherwise would certainly make a positive response.

We all enjoy getting a big hand so you should be delirious with 24 of them in Quizzes 9 & 10.

Quiz 9
MIDMAC 1NT Opener

1. ♠ AQ10x   ♠ KJ9xx
   ♡ AKxx   ♡ xx
   ◊ A   ◊ 10xxx
   ♣ AKxx   ♣ xx

2. ♠ AQxx   ♠ xx
   ♡ x   ♡ KQ108xxx
   ◊ AK10x   ◊ xx
   ♣ AK9x   ♣ xx

3. ♠ K10xx   ♠ xx
   ♡ AQ10   ♡ Kxxxx
   ◊ Ax   ◊ QJxx
   ♣ AK9x   ♣ xx

4. ♠ Ax   ♠ Jxxx
   ♡ Kx   ♡ 10xxx
   ◊ Qx   ◊ Jxx
   ♣ AKQJxxx   ♣ xx

5. ♠ Ax   ♠ xxx
   ♡ Axxx   ♡ KQ9xxx
   ◊ KJ   ◊ xx
   ♣ AKQJ10   ♣ xx

6. ♠ AJxx   ♠ KQx
   ♡ x   ♡ A10xxxx
   ◊ A   ◊ QJ10x
   ♣ AKJ98xx   ♣ -

7. ♠ AKQJ   ♠ 9x
   ♡ AQJxx   ♡ Kxxx
   ◊ AKQ   ◊ xx
   ♣ x   ♣ Q9xxx

8. ♠ AKQJ   ♠ 9x
   ♡ AQJxx   ♡ 8xxx
   ◊ AKQ   ◊ xx
   ♣ x   ♣ KQxxx

9. ♠ AJ10   ♠ Qxx
   ♡ KQJx   ♡ 10xxx
   ◊ AQ10   ◊ Jxx
   ♣ AJ9   ♣ Q10x

10. ♠ K   ♠ J10xx
    ♡ A9   ♡ J8xx
    ◊ AKQ109xx   ◊ xx
    ♣ Qxx   ♣ J10x

11. ♠ A9   ♠ Qxxxx
    ♡ A   ♡ xx
    ◊ Axx   ◊ QJ8x
    ♣ AK9xxxx   ♣ J10

12. ♠ AJxx   ♠ 97x
    ♡ AKQ98x   ♡ x
    ◊ -   ◊ J109xx
    ♣ KQx   ♣ A8xx

Bidding Quiz 10
More MIDMAC 1NT Openers

1. ♠ AQxx   ♠ K8x
    ♡ KQ   ♡ A10xx
    ◇ AKx   ◇ 97x
    ♣ AK10x   ♣ Q7x

2. ♠ AKJx   ♠ Q108xx
    ♡ AQ9x   ♡ J
    ◇ 9x   ◇ Q8xxx
    ♣ AKx   ♣ xx

3. ♠ AK10xx   ♠ xx
    ♡ AKQ   ♡ Jxx
    ◇ AKJ87   ◇ 109x
    ♣ −   ♣ 987xx

4. ♠ AK10xx   ♠ Jx
    ♡ x   ♡ Qxxx
    ◇ A109x   ◇ K8x
    ♣ AKx   ♣ J10xx

5. ♠ KQxx   ♠ J8xx
    ♡ AK10xx   ♡ 9
    ◇ AQx   ◇ J9xxx
    ♣ A   ♣ xxx

6. ♠ AK10   ♠ x
    ♡ −   ♡ A98xxx
    ◇ AK1098xxx   ◇ Qx
    ♣ Ax   ♣ KJ10x

7. ♠ Q   ♠ Axx
    ♡ AKJ9x   ♡ 10xxx
    ◇ Axx   ◇ K9x
    ♣ KQxx   ♣ A108

8. ♠ AJ9xx   ♠ KQ10x
    ♡ AJ9x   ♡ Q10x
    ◇ −   ◇ xxx
    ♣ AK10x   ♣ J9x

9. ♠ AK7xx   ♠ xx
    ♡ AKJx   ♡ 98x
    ◇ −   ◇ Q10xx
    ♣ KJ10x   ♣ AQ9x

10. ♠ AK10x   ♠ Q9xx
    ♡ AQJx   ♡ xx
    ◇ x   ◇ K10xx
    ♣ AJ9x   ♣ 10xx

11. ♠ KJx   ♠ xx
    ♡ Ax   ♡ xxx
    ◇ AKQ9x   ◇ x
    ♣ A9x   ♣ KQ10xxxx

12. ♠ AJ9x   ♠ x
    ♡ AKxx   ♡ J108xxx
    ◇ AKQx   ◇ xxx
    ♣ x   ♣ Axx

Well, I bet you are glad you can now forget about *Intro* and *Houdini* etc. The old weak-style 1NT opener was for masochists. In future you will have a totally new sensation when your partner announces 1NT, viz. relief of anxiety.

However, if you are still troubled by scepticism you may be interested in where the *olde* balanced hands went to when you took up MIDMAC. The following table gives you a quick rundown:

Opener's Bid	Response (CV)		Rebid (CV)	
1♣	1◇ enquiry	6+	1NT	11-15(i)
			2NT	16-17
			3NT	18-19
1 suit	1 major	6+	1NT	11-15(ii)
			2NT	16-17
			3NT	18-19
1 suit	1NT	6-9	Pass	11-15
			2NT	16-17
			3NT	18-19
1◇ 1♡ 1♠	2 minor	10+	2NT	11-13
			3NT	14-16
			4NT	17-19
1NT	2♣	0-7	2NT	20-21
			2NT via 2◇	22-23
			3NT via 2◇	24-25

(i) A further 2 minor rebid by responder asks opener to clarify whether minimum or maximum by minimum or jump NT rebid.

(ii) A further minimum (non-jump) rebid of the initial major response asks opener to differentiate the 11-15 range by minimum or jump no trump rebid.

So the various balanced hands were surprisingly easy to integrate without a natural NT opener. I do not think you will miss not hearing them from your partner at all, but no doubt you will welcome even more the old 1NT from opponents.

• • • • •

With the adrenaline still flowing, I would like to take you into a wonderous cave to demonstrate the comprehensive and exactitude of typical MIDMAC sequences where every bid or rebid has a sensible natural meaning within the defined framework of the original bid, all of which can be worked out at the table. Let us look at, for instance, a sequence that starts 1◇, **2♣**: promising 4+♣ and CV of 10+. We will go through all opener's rebids all the way up to 5♣. Take note of the way the shape of opener's hand invariably becomes defined within one or two options at most.

First the 2♣ responder has a fairly typical:

```
                    ♠ 10xx              CV 12
                    ♡ Ax                Tricks 4+
                    ◇ Qxx
                    ♣ AQ9xx
```

Opener's Rebids	Opener's Hand	Initial Valuation	Responder's Rebid	Responder's Hand
	♠ Ax	CV 11	Pass (5)	10xx
2◇ (4++)	♡ xxx	Tricks 4++	or 3◇	Ax
	◇ AK10xx			Qxx
	♣ xxx			AQ9xx
2♡ (4)	♠ xxx	CV 12	2♠ (4+)	
	♡ KQx	Tricks 4		
	◇ KJxx			
	♣ KJx			

Opener now rebids 2NT promising 3 little spades, with a small doubleton (remember 2♡ denied partial spade stop which includes Qx) opener must have 4 (or conceivably) 5 clubs upon which correction to 3♣ is made. Have you worked out why? That's right, the only other balanced options of a flat hand (3334 type) or 5◇ (3-3-5-2) have already been excluded. Note that on the actual hand opener must be flat with either minor after the 2NT rebid. Incidentally, if opener has maximum 4 trick hand (say ◇A instead of ◇K and therefore an extra control) they would be worth a shot at 3NT, rather than the 2NT rebid.

2♠ (4+)	♠ Q9x	CV 12	2NT (4+)	
	♡ xxx	Tricks 4+		
	◇ AKJx			
	♣ Kxx			

with extra control and vital ♣K, West goes on to 3NT.

2NT (4)	♠ QJx	CV 11	3NT (4+)	
	♡ Qxx	Tricks 4-		
	◇ KJx			
	♣ Kxxx			

Opener's Rebids	Opener's Hand	Initial Valuation	Responder's Rebid	Responder's Hand
3♣(5)	♠ Ax	CV 11	4♣(5)	10xx
	♡ xxx	Tricks 4+		Ax
	◇ KJxx			Qxx
	♣ Kxxx			AQ9xx

Opener declines invitation and passes 4♣ because nothing extra.

3◇(5++)	♠ AQx	CV 16	3♡(5)	
	♡ xxx	Tricks 5++		
	◇ AK10xx			
	♣ Kx			

Responder's 3♡ is clearly showing a stop, not a genuine suit because initial 1♡ response has already been by passed. Opener with 2 spade stops happily converts to 3NT.

3♡(5+)	♠ xx	CV 15	3♠(5)	
	♡ KQx	Tricks 5+		
	◇ AKx			
	♣ K10xxx			

As before, 3♠ asks how useless the unstopped spade suit is. This time, with a little doubleton West converts to 4♣ which East completes to 5♣ game with extra club length and control. Have you worked out that West can only have exactly one shape? That's right specifically 2-3-3-5. Clever, eh?

If you struggle with this type of deduction try sharpening up with Cluedo!

3♠(5)	♠ QJx	CV 14	3NT(4+)	
	♡ Jxx	Tricks 5		
	◇ AKJx			
	♣ Kxx			

3NT(5)	♠ Qx	CV 14	Pass (4+)	
	♡ Qxx	Tricks 5		
	◇ AKx			
	♣ Kxxxx			

Note that opener West doesn't count fit points with this shape. Don't tell me you wouldn't want to be in 3NT given that North didn't overcall 1◇ with 1♠! And even on a spade lead (not more marked than a heart lead) with a 5-3 break you will still make when North underleads AK or a studious South plays the 9 keeping the K or A for the ♠ 10 in dummy. All in all, well in excess of the nominal 50%.

Opener's Rebids	Opener's Hand	Initial Valuation	Responder's Rebid	Responder's Hand
4♣(6)	♠ xx	CV 14	5♣(5)	10xx
	♡ Kx	Tricks 5+		Ax
	◊ AKxxx			Qxx
	♣ Kxxx			AQ9xx
4◊(7)	♠ x	CV 16	4♡(5)	
	♡ Kx	Tricks 5+	Cue	
	◊ AKJxx			
	♣ Kxxxx			

So East/West find their way to 6♣.

4♡(7)	♠ -	CV 15	5♡(5)	
	♡ KJx	Tricks 5	Cue	
	◊ AJ10xx			
	♣ Kxxxx			

Opener despite minimum for 4♡ rebid still bids 5♠ confirming void (East already knows from 4♡ rebid that West had a singleton spade at most) and 0-3-5-5 shape exactly. With ◊KQ East could now sail into 7♣ but as it is subsides in 6♣. If in turn West had ◊K, instead of ◊J10, this one extra vital control would be enough to bid 7♣.

4♠(8)	♠ AQx	CV 19	6♣(5)	
	♡ x	Tricks 6+	or 4NT (KCB)	
	◊ AKJx			
	♣ K10xxx			

East knows that opener is exactly 3-1-4-5 (or conceivably 3-0-5-5) since West did not rebid 4◊, so unless West has extra control (say ♠AKx) 6♣ should be limit. In fact as CT shows, 7♣ is 50%

4NT(6++)	♠ AJ9	CV 18	Pass(4+) but only just!	
	♡ Kxx	Tricks 6++	or 5NT	
	◊ AK10x			
	♣ K10x			

Note that 5NT would here be Quantitative Blackwood saying choose between pass and ace showing response. 6NT would also be mildly invitational! Primarily because West has such great controls and ♣K these two hands in combination produce fair chances for 6NT. I've been in worse!

Give East just one more club instead of a spade and the responder's rebid would certainly be 5NT gladly pushed to 6NT by West. What? Bidding 6NT with only 30 HCP? Shouldn't be allowed!

Opener's Rebids	Opener's Hand	Initial Valuation	Responder's Rebid	Responder's Hand
5♣(7)	♠ Ax	CV 18	5♡(5)	10xx
	♡ Qx	Tricks 6	Cue	Ax
	◊ AKJxx			Qxx
	♣ K10xx			AQ9xx

West now cuebids ♠A and subsides when East rebids 6♣. However, if West had:

♠ Ax	New CV 23
♡ Kx	Tricks 8
◊ AK10xx	
♣ K10xx	

A shot at 7♣ would be quite in order.

If you think I have cheated by giving East a respectable 2♣ response try rebidding all the West hands with East having just about the worst possible 2♣ response.

Say:	♠ Kxx	CV 10
	♡ Axx	Tricks 3+
	◊ Qxx	
	♣ Q9xx	

You will be astounded that you still got to the par spot every time!

If you're still feeling really energetic try constructing your own opener's hands for sequences which start 1◊, 1♡: followed by all opener's rebids up to 4♡. Hopefully you too will marvel at the way opener's hand shape becomes frequently defined exactly, simply because in the first place the 1◊ opener denied 4+ major and 6+ minor hence can only be balanced or two suited in the minors. The secret lies in having specific definition of the opening bid.

You can do similar wonderful things after 1♣ and 2♣/2◊ openers, using the forcing responses. You will find a whole new world of bridge bidding thinking opening up, rather like exploring a limestone cave for the first time and being constantly surprised as you go round every corner. I have one friend (no names, no packdrill) who says it even beats sex, but personally I think that might be going too far, but it's close! It certainly beats sneezing!

3.3 Slam Methods

Slam methods, like supplementary opening bids, are not an integral aspect of the MIDMAC bidding system, but simply an amalgam of the author's preferred ideas. Hence the cohesiveness of MIDMAC is not greatly affected if you have other slam methods that you are proud of and wish to use.

However, to tackle hands in section four you will need to know something about these methods:

1. Key Card Blackwood
2. Cuebids incorporating Trump Ask
3. Quantitative Blackwood
4. Free raise of major to the 5 level
5. 5NT grand slam force

1. Key Card Blackwood
When 4NT is bid immediately after a previous suit bid it is asking for key cards, the king of the previously bid suit counting as an ace. If the asker wants to check for other kings the next lowest bid, other than in the agreed suit, is used for that purpose. The 4NT bidder needs to have at least 1 key card and the responder generally needs at least one ace before being able to show the key king. One exception to this is when the responder's bidding has already denied a hand good enough to contain an ace and a king such as when responding 2♣ to 1NT opener, or having opened with a premptive bid which denies 3 HCP controls.

Responses to 4NT are simple:

	1st Step	2nd Step	3rd Step	4th Step
Keycards	0 or 4	1	2	3

2. Cuebids – incorporating Trump Ask
Once a trump suit is agreed (by direct or belated raise or alternatively after responder to 1 suit has used the same forcing suit response three times) suits with first or second round control (via HCP or shortage) may be bid up the line by either partner, providing at least one first round control is held by each cuebidder.

Once at least one cuebid has been made the use of the lowest level NT bid by either partner is always a trump asking bid (TAB).

The TAB is responded to as follows:

1st Step	2nd Step	3rd Step	4th Step
0 or AKQ	Q	A or K	AK AQ KQ

A further no trump bid by the T.A.Bidder is a simple check back for aces. The bid of the agreed trump suit below game is simply a waiting bid requesting, and leaving room for, partner to show a further 1st or 2nd round control.

Finally, if after TAB with or without subsequent ace check the asker now bids a new suit it expresses grand slam interest depending on partner's holding in this suit in the light of previous bidding. Viz. does partner have more in the suit than already shown, such as:

- 3rd round control when 1st or 2nd have already been denied.
- 1st round control when the cuebid already made showed 1st or 2nd.

One hand will hopefully bring it all together for you:

♠ AQxxxxx		♠ Kxxx	West	East
♡ x		♡ Axxx	1♠(6++)	3♠(5-)
◇ AKxx		◇ xx	4♣(8+)(i)	4♡(i)
♣ A		♣ Jxx	4NT(ii)	5♡
			6◇(iii)	7♠

(i)   cuebids – 1st or 2nd round control
(ii) TAB – East shows K♠
(iii) Grand Slam Probe – since West knows East has A♡ (remember East needs 1st round control to co-operate with cuebidding) all West is interested in is whether East has third round control in diamonds. East, having had the opportunity to cuebid diamonds and having failed to do so is well pleased with the doubleton (the Q◇ would have been OK too) to accept the grand slam invite.

3. Quantitative Blackwood

Since 1NT natural does not exist as an opener it will come as no surprise that MIDMAC features more frequent use of the Quantitative 4NT.

It is suggested that a simple definition will ensure that no further partnerships break up around this issue:

'If 4NT is bid immediately after any NT bid by partner which involved a CV range of more than 2, then 4NT is always Quantitative. If responder has maximum for previous bidding then they show Aces in the normal way. If minimum then they pass.'

Note that 5NT (instead of 4NT) after any NT bid except 4NT would be forcing but still says please bid to show Aces if maximum, otherwise bid 6NT with minimum.

Occasionally, particularly after:

1◊/1♡/1♠, 2 minor: 4NT 6+ tricks, natural + help in responder's minor.

• The 5NT by responder is quantitative but not forcing. Once again opener with maximum shows Aces but passes with a minimum. 6NT instead of 5NT would have mildly invitational overtones too.

Now an example in each category. This is not quantitative because West's 3NT rebid only showed a 2p.t. range. 4NT is Ace ask here:

♠ AQJx		♠ Kxx	**West**	**East**
♡ KQ9x		♡ Jx	1♣(6)	1◊(6+p.t.)
◊ Kx	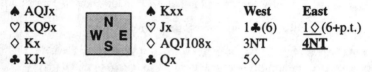	◊ AQJ108x	3NT	**4NT**
♣ KJx		♣ Qx	5◊	

West has shown 4-4-2-3 and 6 trick hand. Incidentally East also knows that for the 6 trick rebid of 3NT, West should have 5 controls so hence must have the other 3 kings.

♠ xx		♠ AK10xxx	**West**	**East**
♡ Kx		♡ Jxx	2◊(5)	2♡(6+)
◊ KQJxxxx		◊ Ax	3◊	**3♠(7)**
♣ Ax		♣ Kx	3NT	4NT
			5◊	6◊

West has shown a 4 or 5 trick hand, with diamonds and heart and club stoppers. With a genuine 5 trick hand (4 controls), West has no hesitation in co-operating to show the hand as a maximum with only one ace. East converts to 6◊. West would have passed 4NT with ♡Qx instead of Kx .

♠ AKQ10xx		♠ xx	**West**	**East**
♡ Qxx		♡ Ax	1♠(6+)	2◊(8p.t.)
◊ Kx		◊ AQJ9xxx	4NT	6NT
♣ Ax		♣ Kx	7NT	

I'll say no more! Well, it's pretty hard to go beyond 7NT though there does appear to be excellent chances for 16 tricks! The importance of the 4NT rebid, promising help in responder's minor, is a clearly crucial feature.

One day perhaps the good bidders will be rewarded by a bonus for overtricks in a grand slam, but until then we will have to be satisfied with 7NT!

4. Free Raise of Partner's Major to the 5 Level
This simply says 'Please go to 6 if your trumps are better than they might be'.

One simple example will suffice:

North/South Game. Dealer South.

			West	East
♠ xx		♠ A	3♡(6p.t.)	5♡
♡ KQ9xxxx	N W E S	♡ 10xxx	6♡	
◊ x		◊ AKQ10x		
♣ xxx		♣ Axx		

I have certainly opened 3♡ at this vulnerability on worse suits. It would be lovely to be able to do the same sort of thing with a minor but sadly I have not discovered how, yet, but we're working on it! Perhaps a 4NT response to a minor pre-empt should say go to 6 with a good suit. Interesting thought ....

5. 5NT Grand Slam Force
5NT as a jump out of the blue after partner's suit bid simply says 'I am interested in something between a small and grand slam, please tell me about honours in your trump holding'. Responses should be in line with those for a TAB.

			West	East
♠ AQJ108xx		♠ Kx	1♠(7+p.t.)	2♣(7++)
♡ KJx	N W E S	♡ A	4♠	5NT
◊ K		◊ A9xx	6♠	7♠
♣ x		♣ AK109xx		

It might only crop up once a year or so but it's still good 'value for memory'.

• • • • •

Please try the hands from Bidding Quiz 2 (p. 50) which seemed so elusive with traditional methods and see if you can now bid them with MIDMAC. Turn to Appendix 1 for the answers.

4
BIDDING:
THE TOPS AND THE TIPS

Introduction

The previous three sections have been to do with providing the bidding building blocks so that they are capable of all fitting together neatly and accurately. This last section, 'Bidding: the Tops and the Tips' is about putting the blocks all together so that you have an overview of the beautiful patterns and highlights, as well as an indication of where the potential for the big swing really lies.

Skill, experience, concentration, judgement, psychology and intuitiveness are all required constantly at the bridge table to avoid costly errors. However, certain bidding situations lend themselves to exploitation as you can look for that special decision that wins matches, tournaments and world championships. You are already showing much more controlled aggression in your bidding but with the solid technical backing and understanding of CV, tricks and controls at hand to prevent you getting altitude sickness. MIDMAC has provided a flexible bidding framework whereby you know much more about the length of critical suits and you can investigate as slowly as you like or bid quickly to the top spot.

These last seven Tops and Tips provide the harmonic climax, a satisfying consummation of all that has gone before, but not the ultimate because my guess is, like so much else in life, we are only looking at the tip or top of the iceberg, but at least we are looking.

Speaking of icebergs, perhaps you have been wondering how a country like Iceland with only a quarter of a million people can emerge out of the cold to win a world championship. I have already, not too subtly, suggested a reason for this, but it seems fitting for our finale to look at bidding of hands from that 1991 World Championship. So the final quiz to see whether you have in fact managed to assimilate and integrate the new concepts presented throughout this book and prescribed more specifically in this section, will focus on hands bid, or rather more frequently misbid, in the 1991 top bridge event. There is, I believe, a hope-for-us-all story in looking at bidding at the top because, as I hope you will discover, you do not any longer need to be in awe of experts. In fact, true expertise in bidding is a very rare commodity, even at the top. You can aspire to do it as well and, joy of joy, with your newly acquired beautiful bidding you will sometimes do it even better.

4.1 Good N = N+1 (Where N = Length of Suit)

It must be very evident to you by now that MIDMAC reinforces, and to some extent revolutionises the principle that a good N suit is equal to, or sometimes better than the same N + 1 suit.

For instance:

- The one major responses to 1♣ and 1♢ deliberately do not differentiate between a good 4 card suit and an ordinary 5 card suit.

- The two major jump response to 1♣ and 1♢ and indeed two minor responses to 1♣ do not differentiate between good 5 and poor 6 card suits; neither do two of a major responses to two of a minor.

- Similarly, three level suit jump responses to all main opening bids (except 1NT) do not differentiate between good 6 or ordinary 7 card suits.

- Other examples where the suit in question is shorter see Tips 4.5 and 4.6.

A hand from the 1989 European Championship where nearly all teams played in 5♣ or 6♣ or 3NT is instructive for our new principle:

♠ AKJ9x		♠ Qx	West	East
♡ Ax	**N**	♡ KQxx	1♠(5+)	2♣(4−)
♢ xx	**W E**	♢ xx	2♠	3♠(5--)
♣ Jxxx	**S**	♣ KQxxx	4♣	4♠

The key bid is West preferring to rebid a great 5 card ♠ suit. Justice would be seen to be done if you found 4♠ because the clubs broke 2-2 and spades 4-2 so there was no defence. Since hearts broke 5-2, 5♣ could not be made even on a non-diamond lead, pointing out the vast superiority of 4♠ as the only viable game contact. As for those in 6♣ or 3NT, what can I say without being harsh?

When we look at hands involving a fit with the suit in question, however, we move into the realms of Moysian fits (4-3) versus 5-3 fits. The primary reason why in MIDMAC, one of a major responses to 1♣ or 1♢ can be made with a good 4+ card suit, is to enable Moysian fits to be found when there is no other viable denomination.

Moysian fits (invariably in a major suit) only produce sound contracts when:

- ruffing value is in the hand with only 3 trumps.
- a substantial minor side suit is available to act as reserve trumps.
- there is a natural resistance to a forcing defence producing early ruffs in the 4 card trump hand.
- the combined 7 card trump suit usually has 3 or all 4 of the top 4 honours if played at game or slam level.

However viable the Moysian fit may be for a particular level of contract, making the good 4 card suit a moderate or poor 5 card suit but otherwise maintaining the trick value of the hand, still almost invariably results in the contract being even more sound, usually by one extra combined trick. In other words, the extra combined trump length is usually worth its extra trick according to CV. Hence responder should still add on one trick if s/he has 5 card suit having promised good 4+.

The conclusion is therefore that the principle of good 4 being equal to 5 is not usually the case when good 3 card support is available.

However, we can conclude with the exception of hands in the Good 3/4 and Good 4/5 category involving Moysian fits, that Good N does equal N + 1 in many situations and sometimes is actually capable of producing an extra trick. This could mean in some situations you do not rebid a poor suit of normally rebiddable length and in others you do rebid a good suit without having extra length. What I hope it really does for you is to get you out of slavish thinking. For instance, one of the difficulties in bidding longer suits without values is that it distorts partner's decision to downgrade for the misfit:

Your partner has opened 1♠ and you have:

> ♠ K9
> ♡ J10xx
> ♢ J87x
> ♣ KQ9

What do you respond?

If you slavishly respond 2◇, the longer minor without the strength, it will be difficult to recover on this perfect double fit hand:

♠ A108xxx   ♠ Kx
♡ KQ   ♡ J10xx
◇ x   ◇ J87x
♣ A10xx   ♣ KQ9

After the 2◇ response West has no choice but to downgrade by a trick and make a quiet 2♠ rebid. It takes a gutsy or intuitive East to now move again especially since the 2♠ rebid does not guarantee 6 on this auction. See what happens though if you use the principle good 3 equals poor 4 and you bid the lower ranking minor. The auction then goes:

West	North	East	South
1♠(5+)	Pass	2♣(3)	Pass
4♣(6+)	Pass	4♠	

Fascinating game, isn't it? Because if you choose to respond 2♣, the minor with the values, it also allows opener's rebids to be more descriptive because there is more room. If opener had been:

♠ A108xxx
♡ KQx
◇ x
♣ A10x

West will rebid 3♠ and you still find 4♠.

4.2 Raising Opener's Suit

The wonderful thing about 5 card majors and 6 card minors, especially when they are opened in first bidding position is that responder with a fit for opener's suit and an unbalanced hand is perfectly placed to make a shaded raise which is both specific in terms of tricks, but at the same time damaging to opponents by taking away their bidding space. Remember when you have a big fit most of the time so do your opponents. Be particularly alert if you think they have the boss suit (spades) fit!

If the 1♡, 1♠, 2♣ or 2◇ opener is made in 2nd, 3rd or 4th bidding position without interference since both opponents have had chance to bid, responder does not have to push so hard to be obstructive but can simply make the value bid. So to summarise:

Shaded Raises	Tricks	Genuine Raises	Tricks
2 level (major)	2/3	2 level (major)	2/3
3 level	4	3 level	5
4 level	5	4 level	6
5 level (minor)	6	5 level (minor)	7

Note with 4 trick hand you can temporise with two minor over one major response or the enquiry response after two minor opening (genuine raises).

The shaded raises do not promise any particular controls, strength or defensive values but simply a suitable inferred trick value including the fit tricks. They are obstructive not constructive.

Typical minimum requirements for shaded major raises made in third position or after opponents have already interfered:

Partner has opened 1♡.

♠ xxx	♠ xxx	♠ xx
♡ Kxx	♡ Kxxx	♡ Kxxxx
◊ x	◊ x	◊ x
♣ xxxxxx	♣ xxxxx	♣ xxxxx

Tricks: 2-3   4   5
Bid: 2♡   3♡   4♡

Two examples from World Championship play will suffice typically and not, incidentally, involving the opening bid in first position:

1. East/West Game. Dealer East.

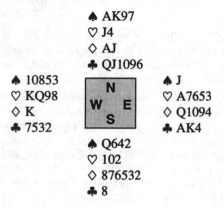

```
                  ♠ AK97
                  ♡ J4
                  ◊ AJ
                  ♣ QJ1096
   ♠ 10853                      ♠ J
   ♡ KQ98        N              ♡ A7653
   ◊ K         W   E            ◊ Q1094
   ♣ 7532        S              ♣ AK4
                  ♠ Q642
                  ♡ 102
                  ◊ 876532
                  ♣ 8
```

Ideal Bidding (for East/West anyway):

East	South	West	North
1♡ (5+)	Pass	4♡ (5--)	All Pass

The combination of 5 card major and shaded raise completely shuts out North and stops North/South finding 4♠ (–1) as a sacrifice.

Now to reverse the vulnerability and the denomination of the opener.

2. North/South Game. Dealer East

```
                    ♠ AJ754
                    ♡ AJ86
                    ◇ –
                    ♣ AK73
      ♠ 10                        ♠ 932
      ♡ 9754          N           ♡ K2
      ◇ QJ87       W   E          ◇ AK9543
      ♣ Q1094         S           ♣ 82
                    ♠ KQ86
                    ♡ Q103
                    ◇ 1062
                    ♣ J65
```

East	South	West	North
2◇ (4+)	Pass	5◇ (5---)	?

West at favourable vulnerability, seeing that North/South have a large number of spades on, bids one more for the road and lurches all the way to 5◇. Poor North is really stuck this time. What would you bid – a desperate 6◇ or simply double? You can see how the 2 minor opening denying 4 + majors enables responder to obstruct even more fiercely than normal.

For your interest, Italy (North/South) had an easy ride to (1) 4♠ and (2) 6♠ respectively and D'Alelio made the slam as well! Some swing!

The 2NT Response
It is all very well raising to the limit and beyond, but what about when responder has a good fit, genuine interest in game and even slam aspirations? The 2NT response, promising 4 + controls including shortage and at least 5 tricks, in other words a genuine willingness to play at the 9 trick level, is available on hands which are too strong for natural suit raises.

This 2NT response applies not only after 1♡ and 1♠ openers but also after 1♣ and 1◇ too, the logical requirement being that responder has an adequate 4+ suit in both majors and minors respectively. The 2NT response, still applies, of course, after the RH opponent has overcalled your partner's 1 suit opening.

The one suit opener after hearing the 2NT response has an easy natural rebid structure:

Opener's Rebid	Tricks*
3 level sign off suit	4
(3 major if 1♣ opener 3 minor if 1◊ opener	
3 major rebid if 1major opener)	
3 new suit natural	5
3NT natural	5
4 level suit (extra trump length included)	5
4 new suit natural	6
4NT natural	6

* Opener's trick valuation excludes the known fit.

Responder if still interested in slam can cuebid or enquire with 4NT key card Blackwood.

It is a real advantage to have a constructive raise particularly when partner has opened in first position:

Game All. Dealer West.

		West	East
♠ J	♠ Axx	1♡(6+)	**2NT**(5+)
♡ AKJ9x	♡ 108xx	4♣(6++)	4◊
◊ A8x	◊ K9x	4♠	5♣
♣ KQxx	♣ A108	5◊	5♡
		5NT	6♣
		6♡	

Here West can immediately see with 7 controls opposite at least 4 that slam is a good bet almost as soon as the 2NT response is made, so even if opponents interfere at a high level in spades it will make no difference to the outcome. Conversely:

East/West Game. Dealer West.

		West	East
♠ A9	♠ KQx	1♡(5++)	4♡(4-)
♡ A10xxxx	♡ K98x		
◊ xx	◊ QJ9xx		
♣ AQJ	♣ x		

Because East's raise denies 4+ controls, West can see that with 9 combined controls maximum slam is not worth investigating. If West does make an informed decision that some catching up is needed, better to raise directly to 6♥ or make a false cuebid in diamonds and hope to avert the dangerous lead.

Let us see the 2NT response in action after all the one suit openers.

♠ AJ9x		♠ KQ10xx	West	East
♥ J10x	N W E S	♥ AQ8x	1♣(4+)	2NT(6+)
◊ x		◊ Axx	3♠	4♣(7)
♣ Axxxx		♣ x	4◊*	4♥*
			4♠	6♠

* cuebids

♠ Axx		♠ 10xx	West	East
♥ xxx	N W E S	♥ -	1◊(5++)	2NT(6)
◊ AQxx		◊ KJ10xx	3NT	4♥*
♣ AQx		♣ KJ10xx	4♠*	5♣
			6◊	

With 2 more controls than promised West can bid 6◊.

♠ x		♠ A10xx	West	East
♥ AQJ9xx	N W E S	♥ Kxxx	1♥(5-)	2NT(7+)
◊ xxx		◊ Ax	4♥(5)	4♠*
♣ KQx		♣ Axx	5♣*	5◊*
			5♥	6♥

* Cuebids

♠ Axxxxx		♠ Kxxx	West	East
♥ J	N W E S	♥ Kxxx	1♠(4)	2NT(6+)
◊ x		◊ Axxxx	3♣(5)	4♠(6-)
♣ KQ10xx		♣ -		

East is not impressed to hear about West's club suit which constitutes a secondary suit misfit because East controls are effectively reduced from 6 to 4.

The 2NT 'strong raise' response concept can also apply after two minor opening in first position. Since the direct raise to 5 level especially non vulnerable can be quite weak in terms of general values and defensive tricks, if you have a genuine raise to five minor (7 tricks with 5+ controls) then the 4NT response is available whether or not the opponents interfere. Opener with an extra two tricks and controls can cuebid looking for a grand slam and with one extra trick and control can bid six of a minor direct.

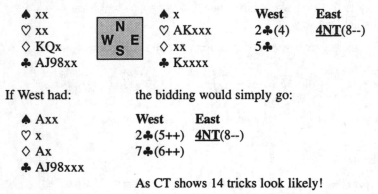

♠ xx	♠ x	**West**	**East**
♡ xx	♡ AKxxx	2♣(4)	<u>4NT</u>(8--)
◊ KQx	◊ xx	5♣	
♣ AJ98xx	♣ Kxxxx		

If West had: the bidding would simply go:

♠ Axx	**West**	**East**
♡ x	2♣(5++)	<u>4NT</u>(8--)
◊ Ax	7♣(6++)	
♣ AJ98xxx		

As CT shows 14 tricks look likely!

4.3 To Jump Strongly or Weakly? That is the Question.

There are many vexed issues and arguments in bridge and this is one of them. For me as responder, my mind has made a quantum leap (or jump shift!) very much in favour of non forcing jump shifts for reasons already outlined in Section 2.3. MIDMAC is therefore rife with descriptive non forcing natural responsive jump shifts, viz.:

Opener	**Jump Responses, typically 5/6 p.t. hand**
1♣	2♡ 2♠ 3♣ 3◊ 3♡ 3♠
1◊	2♡ 2♠ 3♣ 3◊ 3♡ 3♠
1♡	2♠ 3♣ 3◊ 3♠
1♠	3♣ 3◊ 3♡
1NT	3◊ 3♡ 3♠ 3NT(♣)
2♣	3◊ 3♡ 3♠
2◊	3♡ 3♠

So now, having been imbued with the idea that the fast approach involving a jump by responder, immediately or belatedly, is non forcing (and therefore the corollary is that the slow approach involving responder rebidding a suit at the lowest level is forcing), you will be ready to give the complete bidding for the following six responsive hands in conjunction with two opening hands (12 combinations altogether)

Write down the bidding sequence for all 12 hand combinations and then see if your bidding agrees with mine.

Opening hands

	1.	♠ Axxx	2.	♠ Axx
		♡ x		♡ x
		◇ KQxx		◇ KQxxx
		♣ Qxxx		♣ Qxxx

Responder's hands:

	(a)	♠ x	(d)	♠ x
		♡ KQ109xxxx		♡ KQ109xxx
		◇ xx		◇ xx
		♣ Kx		♣ Axx
	(b)	♠ x	(e)	♠ x
		♡ KQ109xxx		♡ KQ109xxx
		◇ xx		◇ xx
		♣ Kxx		♣ AKx
	(c)	♠ x	(f)	♠ x
		♡ KQ109xx		♡ AKQ109xx
		◇ xxx		◇ xx
		♣ Kxx		♣ AKx

1a	1♣	4♡
2a	1◇	4♡
1b	1♣	3♡
2b	1◇	3♡
1c	1♣	2♡
2c	1◇	2♡
1d	1♣	<u>1♡</u>: 1♠, 3♡
2d	1◇	<u>1♡</u>: 1♠, 3♡
1e	1♣	<u>1♡</u>: 1♠, <u>2♡</u>: 2♠, 4♡
2e	1◇	<u>1♡</u>: 1♠, <u>2♡</u>: 3◇, 4♡
1f	1♣	<u>1♡</u>: 1♠, <u>2♡</u>: 2♠, <u>3♡</u>: 3♠*, 4♣*: 4◇*, 6♡
2f	1◇	<u>1♡</u>: 1♠, <u>2♡</u>: 3◇, <u>3♡</u>: 3♠*, 4♣*: 4◇*, 6♡

* Cuebids

You can see in the last two sequences that opener shows complete shape and trick strength and then the third minimal repeat bid of the same suit sets the suit and asks opener to co-operate by cuebidding.

The fast track being limited and the slow track being unlimited is a compelling argument which seems totally logical to me – are you convinced yet?

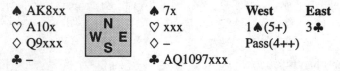

		West	East
♠ AK8xx	♠ 7x	1♠(5+)	3♣
♡ A10x	♡ xxx	Pass(4++)	
◊ Q9xxx	◊ –		
♣ –	♣ AQ1097xxx		

So the worst thing has happened: opener has a void in responder's long suit. No panic because at least you are playing in the best denomination and you have avoided fighting each other and giving valuable information to the opponents in the process. Incidentally, woe betide the opponents if they choose to compete or balance simply because they have balance of power. Contracts of 3◊ or 3♡ (doubled of course) would have more blood on them than a joint of undercooked roast beef (with apologies to vegetarians!). So would my partner (West) if he pulled 3♣ to 3◊!

Two hands from real play might persuade you further:

East/West Game. Dealer South.

		West	East
♠ AKQJ96	♠ 3	1♠(5)	2♡(4++)
♡ Q6	♡ AK98753	2♠	3♡
◊ 10972	◊ –	4♡(6-)	5♣(6)(i)
♣ Q	♣ AJ743	5♡	6♡(6+)

(i)   Cuebid

East is delighted to learn that West does not have a diamond control! It doesn't seem difficult to get to 6♡ with a slow controlled auction as above does it? 7♡ is not quite as good as it looks at first sight. The full hand:

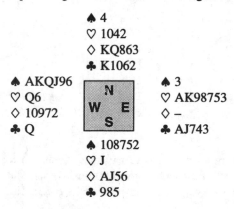

	♠ 4	
	♡ 1042	
	◊ KQ863	
	♣ K1062	
♠ AKQJ96		♠ 3
♡ Q6		♡ AK98753
◊ 10972		◊ –
♣ Q		♣ AJ743
	♠ 108752	
	♡ J	
	◊ AJ56	
	♣ 985	

All four recent World Championship finalists (men and women) failed to reach the only making slam. In fact all played in spades anywhere from four to seven, all contracts going down. Although spade contracts were unlucky to be so punished by a 5-1 break it is a unanimous and not-so-rare indictment of bidding at the top.

Finally, a hand from a Crockford's Cup match which demonstrates how the principle is unaffected by opposition intervention and also takes us into the fascinating area of 4-dimensional thinking, which is the basis of Tip 4.7.

Game All. Dealer West.

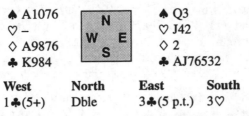

♠ A1076
♡ –
◇ A9876
♣ K984

♠ Q3
♡ J42
◇ 2
♣ AJ76532

West	North	East	South
1♣(5+)	Dble	3♣(5 p.t.)	3♡

The advantage of limit jump responses is evident here. As soon as East responds 3♣ still showing what it would mean without the intervention, West knows that:

1. East/West have 5♣ or 6♣ on depending whether clubs break evenly or not and whether East has 3 hearts (or more) for West to ruff.

2. North/South have an excellent save in a heart contract because it is unlikely that East/West can garner any more than 4 defensive tricks and if they can get the maximum in defence 6♣ for East/West is making.

So what do you bid as West? The full hand and the full bidding:

♠ K9842
♡ KQ108
◇ KJ43
♣ –

♠ A1076
♡ –
◇ A9876
♣ K984

♠ Q3
♡ J42
◇ 2
♣ AJ76532

♠ J5
♡ A97653
◇ Q105
♣ Q10

West	North	East	South
1♣(5+)	Dble(5-)	3♣(5/6 p.t.)	3♡(5--)
4♣(8)	4♡(6)	Pass	Pass
5♣	5♡	Pass	Pass
6♣	Dble	All Pass	

West, with all this 4-D information, sets out to be 'pushed' into 'saving' first with 5♣ and then with 6♣.

Note that it takes very accurate defence for East/West to take 4 tricks against a heart contract, especially if on the ◊A opening lead declarer (South) smoothly plays the Q or ◊10, because after switching to the A♠ at the second trick West is likely to play East for a singleton spade seeing the ♠3 and continue at trick 3 with a small spade. Such deceptively simple declarer play saves two tricks so that the 6♡ save against the cold 6♣ would cost only 200 not 800. (I'm hanging on to my doubled slam though!)

Next time against the same opponents or friends of the same opponents, West would blast to 6♣. It doesn't pay to be too consistently deceptive. It's a great game, isn't it ?

4.4 Minimal Opening Bids

You will realise by now that using CV you are occasionally opening the bidding on shapely hands providing you have at least 3 HCP controls (A and K or 3Ks) with less than your normal quota of overall strength. Do not be afeared, because since we are also devaluing hands for misfit we are quite capable of back pedalling. In fact with MIDMAC we always try to avoid going beyond the level indicated by combined tricks (CT).

For instance with your present bidding methods could you subside in 1NT with?:

♠ 8		♠ AQ9xx	West	East
♡ K109xx	N	♡ Jx	1♡(4)	1♠(3)
◊ KJx	W E	◊ Qxx	1NT(3+)	
♣ KJ9x	S	♣ 8xx		

Experience has indicated that getting into the bidding early and safely, particularly in 1st and 3rd position makes life very difficult for the opponents. At other times the minimal opening bid enables a very good contract to be found that would otherwise be missed. Sometimes it's a gratifying mixture of the two benefits:

North/South Game. Dealer South.

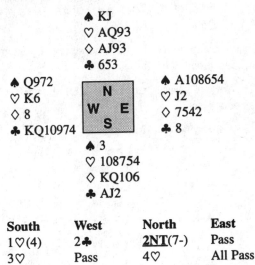

```
              ♠ KJ
              ♡ AQ93
              ◇ AJ93
              ♣ 653
  ♠ Q972                    ♠ A108654
  ♡ K6          N           ♡ J2
  ◇ 8        W     E        ◇ 7542
  ♣ KQ10974     S           ♣ 8
              ♠ 3
              ♡ 108754
              ◇ KQ106
              ♣ AJ2
```

South	West	North	East
1♡(4)	2♣	**2NT**(7-)	Pass
3♡	Pass	4♡	All Pass

4♡ making 5, or perhaps only 4 on a safety play in trumps after K♣ lead. Nothing remarkable in that you might think but in a recent World Championship final this hand was played in 3♣(West) and 4♠(East) without either North or South even having mentioned hearts.

Another rather more subtle reason for opening these minimal hands:

Love All. Dealer South.

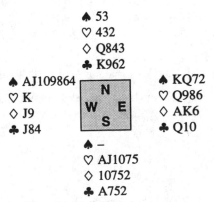

```
              ♠ 53
              ♡ 432
              ◇ Q843
              ♣ K962
  ♠ AJ109864                ♠ KQ72
  ♡ K           N           ♡ Q986
  ◇ J9       W     E        ◇ AK6
  ♣ J84         S           ♣ Q10
              ♠ –
              ♡ AJ1075
              ◇ 10752
              ♣ A752
```

Amazingly in the 1989 World Championship Final both East/West pairs played in 4♠ doubled making for +590 after the following auction:

South	West	North	East
Pass!!(4+)	3♠(6 p.t.)	Pass	4♠(5)
Dble	All Pass		

Both Souths felt compelled to make a reopening double having passed this gorgeous little (almost) 5 trick hand.

In the 1991 World Championship a less subtle reason for opening the bidding was endorsed.

East/West Game. Dealer South.

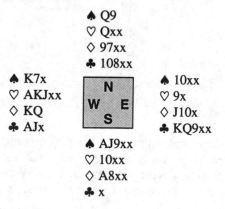

```
                    ♠ Q9
                    ♡ Qxx
                    ◇ 97xx
                    ♣ 108xx
      ♠ K7x                        ♠ 10xx
      ♡ AKJxx         N            ♡ 9x
      ◇ KQ         W     E         ◇ J10x
      ♣ AJx           S            ♣ KQ9xx
                    ♠ AJ9xx
                    ♡ 10xx
                    ◇ A8xx
                    ♣ x
```

If South passes the bidding proceeds:

West	North	East	South
1NT(7+)	Pass	**2♣**(2)	Pass
2♡	Pass	2NT	Pass
3NT	All Pass		

– and indeed nearly all East/West pairs played in 3NT making.

If South instead opens 1♠ on his gorgeous 11 count, East/West have no chance of making 3NT, providing North leads a spade of course.

Game All. Dealer West.

```
                        ♠ Kx
                        ♡ AQ
                        ◇ KQxx
                        ♣ AQJ9x
     ♠ AQ105x                           ♠ J876
     ♡ 98         ┌─────────┐           ♡ K10xxxx
     ◇ x          │   N     │           ◇ 107x
     ♣ K107xx     │ W     E │           ♣ –
                  │   S     │
                  └─────────┘
                        ♠ 9x
                        ♡ Jxx
                        ◇ AJ9xx
                        ♣ xxx
```

West	North	East	South
1♠(4)	Dble(7)	3♠(4)	Pass
Pass	?		

Well what would you bid? Unless it's 3NT you have just lost a bushel of points. If you have doubled 3♠ for penalties you have lost even more because 3♠ is frigid with hearts becoming establishable. In fact the defence will have to be excellent to prevent the overtrick. Are you convinced yet?

Game All. Dealer West.

```
     ♠ 9                              ♠ xxx
     ♡ J97x      ┌─────────┐          ♡ AK8xx
     ◇ A98x      │   N     │          ◇ xx
     ♣ AJ10x     │ W     E │          ♣ K9x
                 │   S     │
                 └─────────┘
```

West	East
1♣(4+)	1♡(3++)
2♡(5+)	3♣(4+)
4♡	

I don't think you will find 4♡ unless you open the West hand. Yes 4♡ does make and 4♠ goes two off (doubled) – not much better for them!

East/West Game. Dealer West.

```
     ♠ A10xx                          ♠ Qx
     ♡ x          ┌─────────┐         ♡ AJ10x
     ◇ A8x        │   N     │         ◇ KJx
     ♣ Q8xxx      │ W     E │         ♣ AK10x
                  │   S     │
                  └─────────┘
```

West	East
1♣(4+)	1◇(6+)
1♠	2♣
4♣(6)	6♣

What a sweet sequence! East knows after West's 4♣ rebid that opener has a 6 trick hand. East has a good 6 tricks so bids to the twelve level.

So, a hand that most people wouldn't dream of opening, becomes worth a genuine 6 tricks after just two rounds of bidding. Tricky stuff!

Penultimately, putting the dampeners on :

			West	East
♠ A10xx		♠ Qx	1♣(4+)	1♡(6+)
♡ x	N W E S	♡ AJ10xxx	1♠(3++)	2♡
◇ A8xx		◇ KJ	2♠	3NT
♣ Q8xx		♣ AKx		

West has shown an absolute (sub) minimum 4-1-4-4 shape with no singleton honour in hearts (2NT rebid would do that), so East realises that the heart suit will take a lot of establishing, so is happy to subside in the obvious game despite the initial excitement.

You do not need to panic if partner starts to look for penalties when you have made your minimal opening. You have as much defence as you promised and you have not opened light – a substantial difference. I remember a hand where the minimal opener had me worried for a while but all was well in the end.

Game All. Dealer West.

♠ AK1087x	N	♠ xx	
♡ 109x	W E	♡ AJx	
◇ x	S	◇ K1097x	
♣ Q9x		♣ Axx	

West	North	East	South
1♠(4)	Dble	Rdbl(4++)	2♣
Dble	2◇	Dble	All Pass

In some trepidation I passed 2◇. My fears were totally unnecessary because the full hand was:

	♠ Q9		
	♡ KQxx		
	◇ AJ8xx		
	♣ Jx		
♠ AK1087x	N	♠ xx	
♡ 109x	W E	♡ AJx	
◇ x	S	◇ K1097x	
♣ Q9x		♣ Axx	
	♠ Jxx		
	♡ 87x		
	◇ Qx		
	♣ K108xx		

We collected a lovely 800. 2♣(doubled) would have netted us 500; all very well compared with our team mates quietly losing 140 to 2♠ making with an overtrick. If North had kept quiet, as I think should happen vulnerable against the mildly pre-emptive 1♠ opening, especially when we are playing penalty doubles against intervention, then we may have played in an aggressive 3NT. That would have been interesting and may well have netted us plus 600. It seems that you can hardly lose with these minimal openers! Notice too that in the last example by defining the West hand as good enough to open 1♠, the weak 2♠ opener becomes more limited in terms of its maximum values hence it is easier for responder to make a decision to pass with a hand such as the East hand.

4.5 Getting into Shape

Opener showing shape either perfectly or with one or two similar related options is an integral feature of MIDMAC after all the main suit opening bids. This is done primarily in one of three ways:

- after responder has used an enquiry bid and then followed with a new suit forcing thereafter on opener to game. (Applies after 1♣, 2♣ and 2◊ openers.)

- after responder has repeated at the minimum level the original minimum level forcing response suit which is also forcing thereafter on opener. (Applies after 1♣, 1◊, 1♡ and 1♠ openers.)

- after a 2 minor response, opener shows shape, with big fitting hands, at the 4 level. (Applies after 1◊, 1♡ and 1♠ openers.)

Let us look how this works after each main suit opener in turn but concentrating on 1♣ and 1◊ openers because these are outstandingly the most frequent.

The L.H. side hand (West) is always opener and as you have already discovered responder (East) with constructive forcing bidding always illicits the shape information from opener.

After a One Club Opener:

♠ AJxx		♠ Kx	West	East
♡ K10xx	N W E S	♡ Ax	1♣(5)	1◊(5+)
◊ –		◊ J109xx	2♣	2◊(6)
♣ KJ9xx		♣ AQ8x	3♣(4+)	6♣(7-)

West has shown 4-4-0-5 shape and 4 trick hand. East is able to visualise the perfect fit in diamonds, viz. poor suit opposite a void, so simply bids to the top spot.

♠ AQ9x		♠ 10x	West	East
♡ K10xx	N	♡ Ax	1♣(5)	1◇(7 p.t.)
◇ K	W E	◇ AQJ10xx	2♣	2◇
♣ QJ9x	S	♣ Axx	3NT	4NT
			5◇	6NT

West shows 4-4-1-4, singleton diamond honour, the King, and a 5 trick hand. (Remember with 4-4-1-4 type with spot card singleton, 1♣ opener will rebid better 4 card major.) East makes a quantitative (non-forcing) Blackwood noise so West confirms maximum but only one ace. East with running 6 card diamond suit has enough to confidently bid 6NT.

♠ AKJx		♠ Q98	West	East
♡ Jxxx	N	♡ –	1♣(4+)	1◇(5)
◇ x	W E	◇ AQxxxxx	2♣	2◇
♣ Kxxx	S	♣ AQx	2♠	4♠(5++)

West shows 4 trick 4-4-1-4 – small singleton diamond with spade suit better than hearts. East appreciates the perfect fit, poor 4 card heart suit opposite a void and all the ingredients for the Moysian fit game. Even on the (obvious) lead of a trump there must be fair chances for 4 minor suit tricks to go with 6 ruffs. On a non trump lead you simply cash two clubs and ace of diamonds early and cross ruff for 10 tricks.

♠ Axxx		♠ K	West	East
♡ –	N	♡ Q1098xx	1♣(5)	1♡(5+)
◇ KQxx	W E	◇ Ax	1♠(4+)	2♡(6)
♣ K9xxx	S	♣ A108x	3♣	6♣(7-)

West shows 4-0-4-5 with only 4 tricks. Again, the void opposite a poor control-less heart suit is the key feature because East knows all West's HCP controls are working. If West had rebid 3◇ showing 4-0-5-4, East would have settled for 5♣.

♠ AQJ9		♠ K10x	West	East
♡ Jxxx	N	♡ AK	1♣(4)	1◇(6+)
◇ xxx	W E	◇ xx	1NT	2♣
♣ Kx	S	♣ AQ10xxx	2♠	3♣
			4♣	4♠/5♣

West has shown 4-4-2-3, 4 trick hand with great spade suit and secondary club support. In pairs East would choose the top 4♠ spot but in teams may be satisfied with 5♣. It's comforting to be able to make the confident choice and avoid the dodgy 3NT in the process.

After a One Diamond Opener:

		West	East
♠ K108	♠ AJ9x	1◇(5)	1♡(4++)
♡ x	♡ Axxxx	1♠(4+)	3♠
◇ AJxx	◇ Kx	4♠	
♣ KJxxx	♣ xx		

After West has shown 4 or 5 trick hand 3-1-4-5 or 3-0-5-5 shape with 3 good spades, East can immediately appreciate with a control rich hand and the heart situation that the only playable game is in spades so invites. Notice that East could simply rebid 2♡ forcing to obtain complete shape and range but this would unilaterally force opener to game level rather than this co-operative approach.

		West	East
♠ AJx	♠ K	1◇(5-)	1♡(4+)
♡ Q	♡ 1098xxx	1♠	2♡
◇ QJxx	◇ Kxx	3NT	
♣ K108xx	♣ AQx		

West shows 5 trick hand 3-1-4-5 with singleton heart honour and good spade suit. East is happy.

		West	East
♠ K10x	♠ xx	1◇(5)	1♡(4+)
♡ K	♡ AQJ9xx	1♠	2♡
◇ K10xx	◇ xx	3NT	
♣ KJxxx	♣ Axx		

West shows again 5 tricks, 3-1-4-5 singleton heart honour hand. East is ecstatic!

		West	East
♠ Axx	♠ x	1◇(5+)	1♡(6+)
♡ x	♡ AK9xxx	1♠(4++)	2♡(7+)
◇ A10xx	◇ Kx	3♣	4NT(8)
♣ KJ10xx	♣ AQ9x	5♠	7♣

West shows 3-1-4-5, 3 key cards including the king of clubs so 7♣ looks odds on. Powerful heady stuff, eh?

			West	East
♠ xxx		♠ xxx	1◇ (5+)	1♡ (5)
♡ x		♡ AKQ109	2♣ (4++)	2♡ (6)
◇ AQxx		◇ K10xx	2♠	3NT(5)
♣ AQ10xx		♣ x		

West shows 3-1-4-5 but no honour in spades, so East knows 3NT is the best viable game spot.

			West	East
♠ Kxx		♠ A	1◇ (5)	1♡ (5++)
♡ –	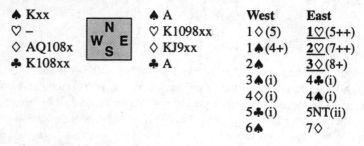	♡ K1098xx	1♠ (4+)	2♡ (7++)
◇ AQ108x		◇ KJ9xx	2♠	3◇(8+)
♣ K108xx		♣ A	3♠(i)	4♣(i)
			4◇(i)	4♠(i)
			5♣(i)	5NT(ii)
			6♠	7◇

- (i) Cuebids 1st or 2nd control
- (ii) TAB

West has shown 4 trick 3-0-5-5 hand with K♠, K♣ and AQ◇. East can simply count 13 tricks by pulling 1 trump only cashing the two pairs of black A and Ks and cross ruffing. Nice to be able to claim before seeing dummy because you have already 'seen' it!

			West	East
♠ AQJ		♠ xxx	1◇ (5+)	2♣ (5+)
♡ xxx		♡ A	3◇	3♡(7)
◇ AJ10xx		◇ K9xx	3NT	4◇
♣ Kx		♣ Axxxx	4♠(i)	4NT(ii)
			5♡	6◇

- (i) Cuebids 1st or 2nd control
- (ii) TAB

West shows 5 trick hand 5-3-3-2 type with 5 diamonds and 3 good spades. West would rebid 3♠ not 3NT if only 3 spades to one honour. After the 3◇ rebid East can already visualise slam in diamonds if opener has good 5 card diamond suit and values in spades rather than hearts.

			West	East
♠ AKx		♠ xx	1◇ (5+)	2◇ (6)
♡ x		♡ AQ10x	4♠ (6+)	4NT(8-)
◇ Q9xx		◇ AK108xx	5♠	7◇
♣ AJ10xx		♣ x		

West shows 3-1-4-5 or 3-0-5-5 with good 3 spades and close to a 7 trick hand. East makes use of KCB (4NT) to get all the information needed to be able to count 13 tricks.

After One Heart/One Spade openers

Opportunities for shape showing are limited but when they do occur its very gratifying.

		West	East
♠ xx	♠ AQ9xxx	1♡(4)	1♠(7+)
♡ AQ10xx	♡ K9x	1NT	2♠
◇ KQx	◇ Ax	2NT	3♡
♣ Qxx	♣ Ax	4◇(i)	4NT(ii)
		5♠	6♡

(i) Cuebids 1st or 2nd control
(ii) TAB

Notice how responder, by rebidding spades at the lowest level, gets into a slow controlled forcing auction which allows West to show 4 trick hand 2-5-3-3 shape ◇K and ♡AQ.

		West	East
♠ AQ9xx	♠ KJx	1♠(6)	2♣(4)
♡ AQJx	♡ xx	4♡(7+)	6♣(5-)
◇ –	◇ xxx		
♣ K109x	♣ A87xx		

West shows 5-4-0-4 and 7+ trick hand. At the 1991 European Championship in Killarney not one pair found the excellent 6♣, showing how ordinary bidding standards are at the top.

After a 1NT Opener

Curiously, the opportunity for shape showing by the big opener are limited because:

- opener tends to be in charge and it is responder who shows values and suits anyway.

- opener's initial shape is unlimited within the various balanced and unbalanced possibilities and statistically shape showing is impossible.

- opener's hand will normally be concealed during the play and it is no longer appropriate to give away such vital information.

However, responder to 1NT occasionally gets close to showing complete shape.

♠ AK	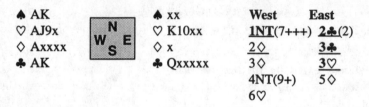	♠ xx	West	East
♡ AJ9x		♡ K10xx	1NT(7+++)	2♣(2)
◇ Axxxx		◇ x	2◇	3♣
♣ AK		♣ Qxxxxx	3◇	3♡
			4NT(9+)	5◇
			6♡	

When responder bids 3♣, a natural 2 trick semi-positive, West, looking at the ♣AK, knows that the club suit is a poor 6 card suit. Subsequently learning about the 4 card heart suit to the King is enough to propel West to slam. Remember the 2♣ responder to 1NT opener is allowed to show the key king, without another ace, following 4NT (KCB).

After Two Club/Two Diamond Openers

♠ AQx		♠ 10	West	East
♡ 10		♡ Qxxx	2♣(5)	2◇(5)
◇ Qxx		◇ AK10xxx	2♠	3◇
♣ AJ10xxx		♣ Kx	4◇(6)	4NT(6)
			5♡	6◇

West shows 3-1-3-6, or conceivably 3-0-4-6, with 3 or 4◇ to an honour. The response to KCB confirms the two aces, enough to shoot out 6◇ on the reasonable assumption that one of the aces is in clubs. If it is not, the slam will require a little bit more but would still be fair.

♠ xxx		♠ xxxx	West	East
♡ x		♡ AQJ9x	2◇(4+)	2♡(5)
◇ AQJ9xxx		◇ K	3◇	3♡
♣ Ax		♣ Kxx	3♠	3NT

West shows a 4 trick hand with 3 little spades 3-1-7-2 or 3-0-7-3; whichever, East can see 3NT is the only viable game.

♠ Axx		♠ xx	West	East
♡ Jxx		♡ AKQ10xxx	2♣(5)	2◇(8p.t.)
◇ x		◇ Axx	2♠	3♡
♣ AKxxxx		♣ x	4♡	4NT
			5♡	5♠
			6♣	7♡

West shows 3-3-1-6 or conceivably 3-3-0-7 with good 3 spades and three poor hearts. The subsequent responses to ace and king asks, confirm the absolute viability of the 'Grand'.

4.6 Undercuts

Bidding a suit naturally when you have already previously denied biddable length or bidding a suit twice when you have already denied rebiddable length are the common examples of undercut in the the MIDMAC system.

It is a most useful device which allows:

- bidding of otherwise 'impossible' hands
- low level escape on misfitting hands
- finding Moysian fits
- 'unusual' no trump contracts to be discovered
- facilitation of shape showing

Undercuts are prevalent on many sequences following the one or two level minor openings.

Let us look at some magical examples after each opening bid in turn:

After a One Club Opener

♠ KJxx		♠ A10x	**West**	**East**
♡ AJ8	N	♡ K9xx	1♣(5)	1◊(4)
◊ x	W E	◊ Q9xx	1♠	2◊
♣ K10xxx	S	♣ Qx	2♡(4+)	Pass

West has clearly a good 3 card heart suit but insufficient tricks to go beyond 2NT to the three (3) level. Note that a 3♣ rebid would have implied a 5 trick hand.

If you improve the controls in both hands you find the only valid game which happens to be in a Moysian fit:

♠ Axxx		♠ xx	**West**	**East**
♡ K10x	N	♡ AJ9x	1♣(5+)	1◊(4+)
◊ x	W E	◊ AJ9xx	1♠	2◊
♣ AQ10xx	S	♣ xx	2♡(4++)	3♡
			3♠(i)	4♡

   (i)   Cuebid

♠ KJ9x		♠ Qx	**West**	**East**
♡ AKJ	N	♡ 10xxx	1♣(5)	1◊(3)
◊ Q8xx	W E	◊ K109	1♠	1NT
♣ Qx	S	♣ K109x	2♡	3NT

Clearly West is showing a 5 trick hand balanced with a great 3 card heart suit. East knows what to do.

| ♠ Axx
♡ K10xx
◇ x
♣ KJ9xx | N
W   E
S | ♠ KJ10x
♡ xx
◇ KQxxx
♣ xx | **West**
1♣(4+)
1♡
2♠ | **East**
1◇(4-)
1♠ |

Clearly East is showing only 4 spades because East did not respond 1♠ initially.

| ♠ –
♡ Axxx
◇ KQxx
♣ A10xxx | N
W   E
S | ♠ J9xx
♡ Kx
◇ J10x
♣ K9xx | **West**
1♣(5+)
1♡
2♡
4♣(6++) | **East**
1◇(3)
1NT
3♣(4-)
5♣ |

West has clearly shown 5 tricks and 1-4-4-4 or 0-4-5-4. East can see the hands fit well so bids on to the great game with little wasted in the spade department. Note also that West is impressed by the fact the East did not rebid 1♠ at the first opportunity.

| ♠ AQ109
♡ 10
◇ AK8x
♣ J10xx | N
W   E
S | ♠ Jx
♡ AQJ
◇ Q97xx
♣ 8xx | **West**
1♣(5+)
1♠
2♠ | **East**
1◇(3)
1NT
3NT(4-) |

This time East has a great heart holding opposite West's shortage so goes for the lowest level game contract.

| ♠ AKQx
♡ 10xxx
◇ xxx
♣ Kx | N
W   E
S | ♠ Jxx
♡ x
◇ AKxxx
♣ Axxx | **West**
1♣(4+)
1NT
2♠ | **East**
1◇(5)
2◇
4♠ |

West is able to show a balanced 4-4-3-2 with a great spade suit and poor hearts so East is able to steer the contract towards spades and away from no trumps.

After a One Diamond Opener

The most common case for the 1◇ opener to show a good 3 card major is of course:

♠ Kxx		♠ QJ9x	West	East
♡ x	N	♡ AJxxx	1◊(5+)	1♡(3)
◊ AQxx	W E	◊ xx	1♠(4++)	Pass
♣ A10xxx	S	♣ xx		

To find such a good and comfortable contract at such a low level is very confidence-boosting. If the opponents decide to back in to the auction West with such good defence would double or redouble to suggest a penalty with which East should be happy to concur.

Similarly, if the opponents overcall 1◊ with a major and partner to the 1◊ opener doubles negatively, it is easy for responder to make a decision knowing that opener can only have 3 of the other major.

♠ x		♠ xxx
♡ A9x	N	♡ KQ10x
◊ KQxxx	W E	◊ xx
♣ Axxx	S	♣ Kxxx

West	North	East	South
1◊(5+)	1♠	Dble(3)	2♠
3♡	3♠	?	

East should now not be tempted to try 4♡ and should be satisfied to try and defeat 3♠, or possibly compete with 4♣ since opener has clearly also shown both minors along with spade shortage and 3 good hearts.

♠ xxx		♠ Axxx	West	East
♡ AJx	N	♡ Q108x	1◊(4++)	2◊(4)
◊ xx	W E	◊ KQxx	2♡	
♣ AKxxx	S	♣ x		

Since West has shown a 4 trick hand with 3 good hearts and no spade stop but otherwise balanced, East is happy to leave well alone.

♠ AJ10		♠ xx	West	East
♡ Qx	N	♡ K10x	1◊(5)	2♣(4)
◊ AQ10xx	W E	◊ xx	3◊	3♡
♣ Qxx	S	♣ AJ1098x	3NT	

West shows a balanced 5 trick hand with 5 diamonds. East's 3♡ bid cannot be seriously suggesting a good 4+ heart suit because East didn't initially respond 1♡. West is happy to bid 3NT knowing the contract is more secure from that side. Note also East knows with guaranteed 8+ club fit the hand is worth 4 tricks.

			West	East
♠ xx		♠ KQ10	1◊ (6)	1NT(2)
♡ AQ10		♡ Jx	3♡	3NT
◊ QJx		◊ 10xxxx		
♣ AKQ9x		♣ 10xx		

West emphasises the great heart suit, although only 3, and West converts naturally to game.

			West	East
♠ AKQ		♠ –	1◊ (6+)	2◊ (4)
♡ 9xx		♡ AJ10x	3♠	3NT
◊ Kxx		◊ 1098xx		
♣ AQ9x		♣ KJxx		

Most pairs would struggle to reliably bid to 3NT on this hand because it is difficult to show a very good 3 card suit without it being construed as 4+.

			West	East
♠ AKx		♠ Jxx	1◊ (4+)	2◊ (5+)
♡ xx		♡ AQ	2♠	3NT
◊ Jxx		◊ AK10xxx		
♣ KJ9xx		♣ xx		

West is able to show a good 3 card spade holding without anything useful in hearts, but otherwise a balanced 4 trick hand. East says 'thank you very much for your undercut.'

After Two Club and Two Diamond Openers

As 2♣ & 2◊ openers both deny a 4 card major, major rebids by opener systematically show a good 3 card suit. The consequence of this is that failure to make an undercut bid denies the requirements for it. For example:

			West	East
♠ xxx		♠ AJ109x	2♣ (5)	2◊ (5)
♡ x		♡ KQ10xx	2NT	3♡
◊ AQx		◊ x	3♠	4♠
♣ AQ10xxx		♣ xx		

West initially denies 3 good hearts or spades by the 2NT rebid when East tries again with forcing 3♡, opener is able to unambiguously show a good 2 or poor 3 spade holding, which is all East needs to hear to have a crack at 4♠. In fact, there is a strong hint that West has 3 little spades (not 2 good ones) because with honour doubleton West may have preferred 3NT.

4.7 Imaginative Bids

So far we have been looking at technical bidding in line with the particular features of MIDMAC and I trust feeling very exhilarated as you discover the system bids give you that extra edge.

Whilst every bid in previous tips and tops may be systematically predictable at least by those who have been playing the system with all its nuances for a few months, this section involves less predictable bids because no bidding system can or should predicate an individuals ability for expansive thinking. So the following tips are designed to separate the magicians from the technicians or mere mortals.

4-D Thinking (one dimension for each direction NSEW)
We are all familiar with 4-D thinking which is frequently necessary to amass clues and deduce inferences when declarer is having to make a crucial play decision but the same sort of thought processes can be applied to bidding. This 4-D thinking seems to involve the ability to 'see' all four hands not just two and to be able to visualise the shapes and key cards therein, without actually needing a long neck and sneaky ways!

However, this sort of thinking does not only apply for playing the hands but is relevant for bidding them except you are trying to 'see' the other three, not two, hands. For instance it is relevant on quite simple hands when trying to judge whether or not to back into the bidding:

Love All. North Dealer.
You (South) have:

♠ AQ9x
♡ x
♢ K109xx
♣ Jxx

West	North	East	South
–	Pass	1♣	1♢
3♣	Pass	Pass	?

Before you decide your next move how can 4-D thinking help ...?

- You are playing a weak 2 major system and the opponents are playing negative doubles of intervention.

1. Since East/West have stopped below game North, your partner, should have some strength; a fair bet would be a 2-3 trick hand.

2. North does not have 3 good diamonds or better because would have pushed with 3◊.

3. Since West did not make a negative double or respond 1♡ or 1♠, West most likely does not hold 4+ in either major.

4. North doesn't have 6+ major because didn't open 2♡ or 2♠.

5. North has short clubs, doubleton at most, because presumably East/West have at least an 8 card fit and with 3 clubs staring at you (South) that leaves a doubleton at worst for your partner.

6. Even if East has 4 hearts and/or 4♠, since West has less than 4 of either major and you (South) have only 1 heart yourself, it looks like North has exactly 5 hearts.

7. So North's shape shape is something like 4-5-2-2 or 5-5-2-1.

Although after all that self-inflicted brain damage you might be regretting not having overcalled 1♠ at your first turn it looks fairly safe now to back in with 3♠, especially at pairs.

Note incidentally, TNT would also suggest that since East/West have 8+ card club fit so most likely do North/South have an equivalent fit with the spade suit being the obvious denomination.

The full hand was:

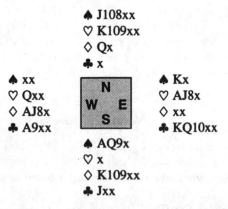

                    ♠ J108xx
                    ♡ K109xx
                    ◊ Qx
                    ♣ x
    ♠ xx   ┌─────────┐   ♠ Kx
    ♡ Qxx   │   N   │   ♡ AJ8x
    ◊ AJ8x   │ W   E │   ◊ xx
    ♣ A9xx   │   S   │   ♣ KQ10xx
                    └─────────┘
                    ♠ AQ9x
                    ♡ x
                    ◊ K109xx
                    ♣ Jxx

On careful play both black suit part scores can just make 9 tricks.

The opportunity for this sort of thinking is frequent and when applied on more crucial big hands is a potential source of enormous gains.

Take this seemingly innocuous hand:

Game All. Dealer North.
You (South) hold:

♠ J109
♡ Axxx
◇ xxx
♣ Qxx

Bidding (North/South MIDMAC)

West	North	East	South
–	2♣	Pass	Pass
2◇	3♣	Pass	Pass
3♠	Pass	Pass	?

Again you (South) are in the spotlight for some 4D brain disintegration. What do you know from the bidding to date ...?

1. West did not double initially but vulnerable produced first a 2◇ overcall then 3♠, so clearly is a maximum for non doubling action but with presumably only 4 good spades to go along with good 5+ diamond suit. With 5+ spades West would presumably have firstly overcalled 2♠.

2. North had shown extra strength and a good 7+ clubs but because North didn't reopen with 2♡, 2♠ or a double does not have 3-3-0-7 shape or a good 3 card major at all. 4♣ must be a safe competitive bid with CV of the South hand increasing now to 12 (4-tricks). You can guess North is 1-2-3-7 or 2-2-2-7 in fact.

3. East has left 3♠ so has much better spades than diamonds.

Being a person who likes to have your cake and eat it, can you think of an imaginative bid that can hardly lose ...? Of course, 3NT! If North's hand is unsuitable like a club suit without 2 of the top 3 honours you can trust partner to pull to 4♣ knowing 3NT must be based in part on your club support. Note also that 3NT rather than 4♣ makes it more difficult psychologically for East/West to move again to 4♠, a most interesting contract to play as you can see:

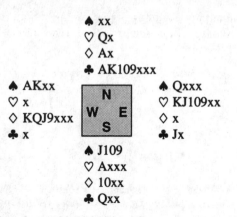

```
                    ♠ xx
                    ♡ Qx
                    ◊ Ax
                    ♣ AK109xxx
    ♠ AKxx              N              ♠ Qxxx
    ♡ x          W          E         ♡ KJ109xx
    ◊ KQJ9xxx          S              ◊ x
    ♣ x                                ♣ Jx
                    ♠ J109
                    ♡ Axxx
                    ◊ 10xx
                    ♣ Qxx
```

Your reputation is enhanced by admiring glances as you wrap up 3NT and try to calm your swelling ego. This 4-D thinking is pretty good stuff. The kibitzers think you are some sort of Guru and you are not going to disillusion them.

The Only Bid
The Italians, in their heyday, introduced the concept of controlled aggression in their bidding. Rixi Marcus was renowned for a bold, although often technically unsound approach to bidding which sometimes was justified only by the fact that the opponents forgot to double.

Beautiful bidding should be the best of these principles and is all about choosing the right bid for the right moment, technically and tactically sound taking into account all the evidence. Jannersten talked about the 'Only Chance' when playing the cards. I think the word *'only'* could also be applied to the choice of bid. The challenge of this tip is to find that exclusive precious bid; the bid that has just the desired effect. One bridge novice found the *only bid* early in his playing days:

The novice was playing with the club chairperson for the first time and enquired nervously about the likelihood of picking up all 13 cards of the same suit. The rather officious chairperson said, 'Don't worry about that – if you ever got 13 cards in the same suit you can make love to my spouse.' On the second hand the novice inevitably fans out the cards and sees, one by one, all 13 spades. The novice leaned over to the chairperson and said 'by the way is your spouse here?' The chairperson pointed to an incredibly ugly creature sitting all alone in the corner of the room. The novice, on being reminded that s/he was dealer quietly said 'no bid'.

We all know about the gambling 3NT as an opener but the use of 3NT as a gambling response is much undervalued, especially after 1◇, 2♣ and 2◇ MIDMAC openers.

Adventurous players are, or should be, prepared, especially at teams, to raise a weak 1NT opening to 3NT in 3rd position with:

♠ Kx
♡ Kx
◇ KQxxxxx
♣ xx

Extending the idea you are playing MIDMAC and your partner has opened 1◇. What do you respond non-vulnerable in third position with:

♠ Kx
♡ Jx
◇ KQxxxxx
♣ xx

Well since your partner has denied 4+ major/s it looks like if your partner is minimum, that opponents have some sort of major game contract on. 3◇ non-forcing might be the book bid but in third position 3NT is much more likely to impede the opponents.

The full hand:

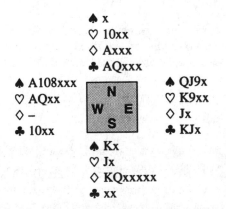

```
              ♠ x
              ♡ 10xx
              ◇ Axxx
              ♣ AQxxx
♠ A108xxx    ┌─────────┐    ♠ QJ9x
♡ AQxx       │    N    │    ♡ K9xx
◇ –          │ W     E │    ◇ Jx
♣ 10xx       │    S    │    ♣ KJx
             └─────────┘
              ♠ Kx
              ♡ Jx
              ◇ KQxxxxx
              ♣ xx
```

On the normal spade lead 3NT rolled home whilst 6♡ or 6♠ happened to be on for the opponents. Note that 3NT could not really lose because if West made a confident double you could consider retreating to 4◇ knowing partner has at least 2.

Again playing MIDMAC you (West) note partner (East) open 1♠ in 1st position at favourable vulnerability. How do you respond after RHO doubles, with this Yarborough:

♠ 95432
♡ 983
♢ 7
♣ 6543

The only bid to make life really difficult for the opponents is the red blooded stretch to 4♠. The full hand:

♠ Q
♡ Q42
♢ 6432
♣ QJ1097

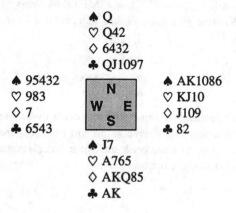

♠ 95432   ♠ AK1086
♡ 983   ♡ KJ10
♢ 7   ♢ J109
♣ 6543   ♣ 82

♠ J7
♡ A765
♢ AKQ85
♣ AK

Anything less would give opponents chance to bid and make 5♢ (by process of loser on loser play if East/West start with two top spades), whilst 4♠ only goes one off as predicted with CCV of 24 for East/West.

Give opponents enough rope in the bidding and they can hang themself (or 'Ropey' bids for short).

With a bit of 4D imagination you can think about finding the only bid that may mislead the opponents when they are trying to decide which is their best contract.

But first another related tip:

If you are outgunned it is often puerile to raise partner's suit when you have no chance of going anywhere.

North/South Game. Dealer West.

```
                    ♠ J4
                    ♡ J1032
                    ◇ A32
                    ♣ AJ92
    ♠ A96                        ♠ 53
    ♡ AQ654          N           ♡ K987
    ◇ Q74         W     E        ◇ K1065
    ♣ K8             S           ♣ 765
                    ♠ KQ10872
                    ♡ –
                    ◇ J98
                    ♣ Q1043
```

West	North	East	South
1♡ (5+)	Pass	2♡ (3)	2♠
3♡	3♠	Pass	4♠

East's raise to 2♡ is standard assuming opener only has 4 hearts, although already East must be wondering about the opponents spade contract and at this vulnerability and bidding position could and perhaps should against good opponents consider something else. However, West is the real culprit for bidding again (3♡) which makes South's heart void become even more useful.

If West passes at second turn, and North tries 3♠, I do not think many South's would now have a shot at 4♠.

Note, also that this hand also shows the advantage of 5 card majors since East would then be worth a shaded raise to 3♡ and it would now take a brave South to come into the bidding vulnerable at the first opportunity to speak.

However, back to the point, the bidding has gone:

West	North	East	South
1◇	1♡	1♠	?

Love All. Dealer West.
You (South) have:

```
                    ♠ K107
                    ♡ 9732
                    ◇ 108
                    ♣ K1082
```

What do you do and why …?

If you simply raise to 2♡ or even an aggressive 3♡, competent opponents will be able to judge to bid 4♠ but if you disguise the heart support and bid 1NT they may misread both the major suit layouts and prefer 3NT.

In fact at the table against a most seasoned Sheffield pair the bidding proceeded:

West	North	East	South
1◊	1♡	1♠	1NT
Dble	Pass	3♠	Pass
3NT	All Pass		

The full hand:

```
                 ♠ 65
                 ♡ AJ654
                 ◊ A53
                 ♣ 754
   ♠ A                         ♠ QJ98432
   ♡ Q8          N             ♡ K10
   ◊ KQJ9762   W   E           ◊ 4
   ♣ AJ6          S            ♣ Q93
                 ♠ K107
                 ♡ 9732
                 ◊ 108
                 ♣ K1082
```

The outcome was a very satisfactory 3NT–1 against 4♠ making for our East/West in the other room. For South to bid 1NT was a cost-nothing maybe gain-everything ploy, a repeating feature of the 'Only Bid'.

Third Hand Bidding

I might be out on a limb sometimes but when I read month after month in the E.B.U. magazine *English Bridge* all this 'tripe' about psyching I almost get the feeling that the *English Bridge* fraternity have developed a chronic case of paranoia and I feel like having a quiet 'chunder' in the corner!

• • • • •

I recall one hand early after my return to U.K. in 1989 playing in my local club in a pairs event where third in hand non-vulnerable, I contemplated my bid after two passes staring at:

♠ K
♡ Kxx
◇ KQ10xx
♣ J10xx

Well, the first question that should spring to mind when you have the benefit of knowing your partner does not have opening values is to try and decide what the opponents might have on. I decided in view of my poor major holdings that they may well have a contract in hearts and/or spades.

The next decision was to find a bid that was right for us and wrong for them. In other words, a safe bid that would make life difficult for opponents. MIDMAC was not even a twinkle in my eye in those days so I naturally chose 1NT, got the expected spade lead and wrapped up 7 tricks when they had 110 or 140 playing in 2♠. At the end of the hand there were grave muttering when it was discovered I only had one spade in my hand and I was told quite firmly that I couldn't open 1NT with a singleton. I got my name put in the psych book for simply choosing the appropriate tactical and technical bid.

So I would like to start a revolution and state that in third position, particularly at green vulnerability, it is not really an issue of psyching but simply trying to find the optimum bid having drawn conclusions from the bidding thus far. Is that not what you should be trying to do all the time?

I would be quite happy for my partners to alert all my third hand 'green' bids or overcalls and say if asked 'Beware my partner has been guilty in the past of choosing some offbeat bids in this position'. Whether it is strictly alertable considering that I would expect any thinking and imaginative player to do the same against me, would get us into quite an interesting debate and keep the *English Bridge* letters to the editor pages overflowing for the next year or two.

Going back to my 'disgraceful' bid, it is worth noting that following the principle that a singleton honour is as good as a small doubleton (see 4.1) the value of having rules that define a psych as 'opening 1NT with a singleton' become even more questionable. Like most bureaucracies in providing necessary boundaries there is a real danger of stifling imagination and initiative (in bidding ideas).

So you might, rightly, be getting the idea that these third hand bidding tips are not for the fainthearted but they are definitely for the 'faintspaded':

Your partner has opened 2♡ weak and you have:

Love All. Dealer West.

> ♠ J93
> ♡ K753
> ◊ Q10832
> ♣ 6

What do you do? Back to the golden rules of this tip:

1. Try to work out what the opponents may have on.
2. Try to find a bid to make it difficult for them to realise their desserts.

Well, on this hand you know that they have game or slam on in one of the black suits. What power to know that when they don't yet! So East's choice of bid should be primarily obstructive or even destructive but not particularly constructive.

Your choice of options depending on how you judge your opponent's style and ability are multifarious, ranging from pass to some high level of hearts but also including the devilish 2♠ (non forcing and perfectly safe) 2NT or 4NT. Fascinating game, isn't it? For me the only bid is 2♠ but this is one situation where there might be quite a few 'only bids'.

Partner (Dealer) has opened 2♠ (weak) favourable vulnerability you hold:

> ♠ Axx
> ♡ Q109x
> ◊ xxx
> ♣ Qxx

After pass by RHO you have a decision to make. What is it?

Well, normally you would not dream of responding with this flat hand particularly when opener might have only 5 spades but this situation is not normal. You know the opponents may well have game somewhere if opener is minimum, so perhaps it's worth trying to put pressure on with either 2NT or 3♠. The full hand was:

North/South Game. Dealer West.

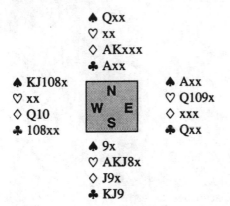

```
                    ♠ Qxx
                    ♡ xx
                    ◇ AKxxx
                    ♣ Axx
    ♠ KJ108x          N           ♠ Axx
    ♡ xx                          ♡ Q109x
    ◇ Q10        W       E        ◇ xxx
    ♣ 108xx          S           ♣ Qxx
                    ♠ 9x
                    ♡ AKJ8x
                    ◇ J9x
                    ♣ KJ9
```

Yes, opener is pretty putrid and you could go for heaps in 3♠ doubled but how are they going to be able to do that? My partner (East) passed at the table and South balanced with 3♡ and 3NT was bid and made by North. A chance wasted because 3♠ or 2NT probably would have been just enough to deter North/South from getting into the action.

When bidding in third position I have much in common with Adam 'Plum' Meredith who was a man who knew when to call a spade a spade and sometimes anything else a spade as well! It is always a good idea to look at your spade suit carefully before deciding your bid in third position:

After two passes at Love All what do you open with:

> ♠ A3
> ♡ AQ109843
> ◇ Q
> ♣ J108

Only one lady in the 1989 European Ladies Championships found 4♡. The full layout was:

Love All. Dealer North.

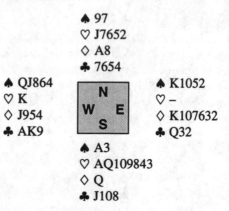

```
                      ♠ 97
                      ♡ J7652
                      ◇ A8
                      ♣ 7654
      ♠ QJ864                      ♠ K1052
      ♡ K              N           ♡ –
      ◇ J954        W    E         ◇ K107632
      ♣ AK9            S           ♣ Q32
                      ♠ A3
                      ♡ AQ109843
                      ◇ Q
                      ♣ J108
```

I think she deserved the enormous swing which resulted when 4♡ actually made at her table on a misdefence whilst 5♠ (East/West) made at her other table also on a misdefence.

The point is that rules are meant to be broken or at least bent considerably and to open 1♡ is to allow opponents in to bid the boss suit, spades, a much more important consideration than pre-empting with two aces.

Lest this book get into the hands of minors I will desist on giving specific examples of when it is appropriate to bid or overcall a fictitious spade suit but I would seriously consider it anytime non vulnerable in third position when:

• I do not have a genuine constructive bid
• I do not have much defence
• I have some reasonable 5 + suit
• I have at least three spades and ruffing value

Beyond that my lips are sealed!

• • • • •

After all those Tops and Tips you might now, like Topsy, be feeling a little tipsy, so have a rest and when you have recovered you might like to try Quiz 11 which gives a refresher on ideas presented in Section 4.

Quiz 11 – Bidding

All these hands were taken from the 1991 World Championships and involved typically half or more of the field making less than optimum bidding decisions. They have also been selected to demonstrate the concepts raised in Section 4. If you and your partner manage to bid half of them correctly you are already bidding as well or better than those at the top of their countries at least sitting in an armchair rather than in the pressure cooker of bridge at the top.

The hands have been rearranged so West is always the first to open unless otherwise stated. Interference where it realistically occurred at the table is also given to try and replicate actual bidding condition. Good luck. Optimum MIDMAC sequences with some commentary is provided in Appendix 1.

Vulnerability is included where it might affect the bidding decisions.

1. East/West Game

♠ A10xx	♠ KQ
♡ AKx	♡ xxx
◇ AJ8	◇ KQ10xxx
♣ K9x	♣ xx

2. East/West Not Vulnerable

♠ 8	♠ AQ10xxxx
♡ KQ876	♡ 9x
◇ K108xx	◇ J9x
♣ AQ	♣ x

3. Love All

♠ 8x	♠ AQ10x
♡ K9x	♡ A8x
◇ QJ10	◇ A987xx
♣ AJ87x	♣ –

4.

♠ AJ108xx	♠ x
♡ Axx	♡ Jx
◇ 97	◇ Axx
♣ J10	♣ AKQxxxx

5.

♠ Q	♠ AKJ97
♡ A9xx	♡ Q10
◇ AJxx	◇ Kx
♣ AQ8x	♣ Jxxx

6.

♠ Q	♠ AK109xxx
♡ AQx	♡ Kxx
◇ A10xx	◇ x
♣ AJ9xx	♣ Kx

7.

♠ AKJ	♠ –
♡ A109x	♡ Qx
◇ AQ	◇ J1087xx
♣ Qxxx	♣ A108xx

8.

♠ Kxx	♠ AQ9
♡ x	♡ QJxx
◇ KQ9xx	◇ AJ10x
♣ AK10x	♣ xx

9.

♠ A9xx	♠ x
♡ 10x	♡ xx
◇ 8x	◇ AKJ10xx
♣ AQ98x	♣ Kxxx

10.

♠ AJ10xxx	♠ Kxxx
♡ J10	♡ AKQ9xxx
◇ Ax	◇ Qx
♣ Jxx	♣ –

11. North overcalls 2♣

♠ A10987	♠ KQJxx
♡ Ax	♡ KQ109
◇ AJx	◇ 10xxx
♣ K10x	♣ –

12. North overcalls 2♡

♠ A87xxx	♠ KQxx
♡ Qx	♡ –
◇ x	◇ J1098
♣ A97x	♣ KQ10xx

13. North overcalls 2♠
South raises to 3♠

♠ –	♠ AQx
♡ A1098x	♡ Jxxx
◇ AJxxx	◇ Kx
♣ AJx	♣ K10xx

14.

♠ A10xx	♠ QJx
♡ Ax	♡ xx
◇ Jx	◇ K98xx
♣ AKQ87	♣ J10x

15.

♠ AKJ9xx	♠ Q10xx
♡ J8x	♡ A9
◇ Ax	◇ KJ8xx
♣ Ax	♣ 9x

16. Game All

♠ K10x	♠ A8xx
♡ KJ87xx	♡ A9x
◇ xx	◇ Kxxx
♣ A10	♣ xx

17. East/West Game

♠ Axx	♠ QJ9x
♡ x	♡ AJ9xxx
◇ KJ108x	◇ AQ
♣ K9xx	♣ x

18. South as dealer opens 1◇

♠ 109xx	♠ Ax
♡ Jx	♡ AKQ1087x
◇ J10x	◇ Qxx
♣ A8xx	♣ x

Would it matter if South opens 1♣?

19. East/West Game

♠ Kxx	♠ Q109876x
♡ Kxx	♡ Jx
◇ x	◇ 10xx
♣ AQJ8xx	♣ K

20.

♠ Ax	♠ Kxx
♡ Axx	♡ KQJ10xx
◇ 10xxx	◇ J
♣ KQ10x	♣ A9x

21.

♠ AQxx	♠ KJ10x
♡ AQ98xx	♡ x
◇ Ax	◇ K98
♣ J	♣ K108xx

22. Game All. Dealer West

♠ xx	♠ Qxx
♡ Ax	♡ 108x
◇ Kx	◇ 10xxx
♣ KJ109xxx	♣ AQx

23

♠ K10x	♠ J9xxx
♡ AKQJ9x	♡ x
◇ Ax	◇ KJx
♣ KJ	♣ 107xx

24.

♠ K10	♠ AQx
♡ A8x	♡ Q7x
◇ KJ9	◇ A107xxxx
♣ K9xxx	♣ –

• • • • •

If you have stayed the pace, I hope you have found the journey breathtakingly beautiful if not a little gruelling. All you need now is a partner and you are in business. Whilst deciding whether to take on board MIDMAC remember that with CV and your new mindshifts you will certainly improve dramatically because you have become an open minded thinker.

Although it is said that anticipation is greater than arrival I would add that in bridge, as in life, we never arrive; the best we can hope for is to enjoy and learn every step of the way.

If you have already been convinced to try MIDMAC, a word of warning rather akin to the old TV image breakdown message:

'Do not adjust the system; the fault lies in the receiver!'

Whatever, I sincerely hope the presented ideas stimulate you sufficiently to create a new wave of enthusiasm for the game because we all need inspiration to appreciate the beauty that surrounds us.

As someone very dear to me once said – a little gem, a treasure which came out of darkness.

'I would rather be a dreamer than a no-hoper.'

May your beautiful bidding go with you.

APPENDIX

Answer to All Quizzes
(Tricks in parenthesis –
Forcing bids in bold and underlined. Playing tricks shown by p.t.)
(i) and (ii) in the appendix indicate the following: (i) Cuebid (ii) TAB

Answers to Quiz 1 Tricks and Controls

'Benjy' Acol.

1.

West	East
1♡(6)	**1♠**(2+)
3♣(6+)	4♡(3+)

West must have spade tolerance to still have 6 trick hand otherwise it would be downgraded by a trick. East can upvalue by a 'good' trick because of the 8 card heart fit, good controls and no wasted values in diamonds opposite West's known shortage.

2.

West	East
1♠(4+)	2♠(3)
4♠(7)	

3.

West	East
1♠(5-)	2♠(3)
Pass(6--)	

4.

West	East
1◊(5+)	**1♡**(3+)
3♡(6)	4♡(4)

5.

West	East
1♣(6)	**1♠**(4)
4♠(7)	6♠(5)

West must have at least 6 controls for 7 trick rebid therefore East 'seeing' at least 10 controls in combination goes for slam.

6.

West	East
1♠(6+)	2♠(2)
4♠(8)	

7.

West	East
Pass(4-)	1◊(5)
2♡	4♡(6++)

West does not have enough controls to open this borderline hand. East though, who has 7 controls opposite West's presumed 2, is not deterred from raising the 2♡ response to game. Incidentally, East knows West must have good 5 hearts or conceivably 6 hearts and 4 spades because West did not initially open 2♡.

8.

West	East
1♠(5)	2♠(4-)
2NT(5)	**3♡**
3NT	

West does not have enough controls to go to the 3 level. East knows that controls for 4 level are insufficient.

9.	West	East
	1♣(6)	1♠(2)
	2♣(5)	3♣(3+)
	5♣(7)	

East's great controls push the hand to 3+ tricks.

10.	West	East
	1◇(5+)	1♡(3++)
	3♡(6+)	4♡

11.	West	East
	1♠(4)	1NT(3–)

East does not have enough tricks with only 1 control for the 2 over 1 response because the East hand is downgraded by 1 trick.

12.	1♡(4)	2◇(7++)
	3◇(4+)	4NT(8+)
	5◇	5NT
	6◇	

Yes, West is worth a 1♡ opener with 3 controls to go with the 4 trick hand. Once West makes a sensible rebid of raising diamonds East's only decision is whether 6◇ or 7◇ is optimum. If you got this one night you did better than most who bid the hand in a recent world championship!

Answers to Bidding Quiz 2 – Ideal Final Contracts (Acol Bidding Test)

(1) 1♡	(2) 1NT	(3) 4♡
(4) 4♡	(5) 4♠	(6) 4♡
(7) 4♠	(8) 6♣	(9) 2◇
(10) 2♡	(11) 3♠	(12) 6NT

If you had difficulty with these hands read on into Section 3 ... If you didn't, can I please have a game with you sometime?

MIDMAC Bidding Sequences for Bidding Quiz 2

1.	West	East
	1♣(5++)	1◇(3)
	1♡	Pass

2.	West	East
	1♣(4+)	1♠(3)
	1NT	

3.	West	East
	1◇(5)	1♡(5++)
	2♡(5+)	4♡

4.	West	East
	1◇(4+)	1♡(4++)
	2♡(5)	3♡
	4♡	

5.	West	East
	1♣(5++)	1◇(3-)
	2♠	4♠(4-)

6.	West	East
	1♣(6-)	1◇(3+)
	1NT	3♡(4)
	4♡	

All high cards in East hand are pulling weight.

7.	West	East
	1♣(5+)	1◇(4+)
	1♡	1♠
	3♠	4♠

8.

West	East
1♣(4)	**1♢(5++)**
2♣	6♣(8)

9.

West	East
1♢(5)	**1♠(3+)**
2♣(4)	2♢(4)

10.

West	East
1♣(5+)	**1♠(3)**
2♣	2♡

11.

West	East
1♡(4)	**1♠(4+)**
2♣(3)	3♠(6 p.t.)
Pass(3–)	

12.

West	East
2♢(5)	**2♡(6++)**
2NT	4NT(Quant)
6NT	

Answers to Bidding Quiz 3 – MIDMAC 1♣ Openers

1.

West	East
1♣(5+)	**1♢(2+)**
1♠	Pass

2.

West	East
1♣(5+)	**1♢(4+)**
1♠	3♠(5)
4♠	

3.

West	East
1♣(5)	**1♠(3)**
2♠	

4.

West	East
1♣(6+)	**1♢(3)**
3♣	4♠(4)

5.

West	East
1♣(5+)	**1♢(4)**
1NT	2NT
3NT	

6.

West	East
1♣(4)	**1♡**
1NT	3♡(6 p.t.)

The jump rebid by responder or indeed any jump suit by responder in the Midmac system is not forcing. West has no more than already promised to consider 3NT or 4♡.

7.

West	East
1♣(5+)	**1♡(4)**
2♣(4++)	Pass

8.

West	East
1♣(5+)	**1♠(2)**
2♠	

9.

West	East
1♣(5++)	2♠(4+ p.t.)
Pass(5++)	

10.

West	East
1♣(5++)	2♣(5 p.t.)
2NT	3NT

or

1♣	3♣
3NT	

Remember 2 of a suit and 3 of a suit responses to 1♣ are not forcing.

11.

West	East
1♣(4+)	**1♡(4–)**
1♠	2♣

12.

West	East
1♣(6+)	**1♠(2+)**
2♡(5+)	Pass

Answers to Bidding Quiz 4 – MIDMAC 1♣ Openers

1.

West	East
1♣(5+)	<u>1♢</u>(4)
2NT	3NT

Opener has CV of 16 with good spots and excellent controls.

2.

West	East
1♣(6+)	<u>1♠</u>(5+)
4♣(7+)	<u>4NT</u>(KCB)
5♠	5NT
6♢	7♠

3.

West	East
1♣(5–)	<u>1♡</u>(5+)
2♢	<u>4NT</u>(6+)(KCB)
5♢	

4.

West	East
1♣(5–)	<u>1♡</u>(4)
2♢(4)	2NT
Pass	

5.

West	East
1♣(6++)	2♠(4+ p.t.)
6♠(9+)	

Virtually good enough for 1NT opener. Opener knows East has 6 card suit because he cannot have good 5.

6.

West	East
1♣(4+)	<u>1♢</u>(3+)
1NT	2♡

7.

West	East
1♣(4+)	<u>1♢</u>(4+)
1♠	<u>2♣</u>
2♢	2NT
3♢(6)	4♢(5+)
5♢	

East's controls and potential ruffing value make 4♢ try worthwhile.

8.

West	East
1♣(5)	<u>1♢</u>(4+)
2♢	4♢(5+)
5♢(6)	

9.

West	East
1♣(5+)	<u>1♡</u>(7 p.t.)
1NT	<u>2♡</u>
4♡(6)	<u>4NT</u>(KCB)
5♡	6♡

10.

West	East
1♣(5)	<u>1♠</u>(4 p.t.)
1NT	2♠
3NT	

11.

West	East
1♣(6)	<u>1♢</u>(5+)
2♡	<u>4NT</u>(6)(KCB)
5♠	6♡

Note that with ♣K instead of ♣A West would not have enough controls for 2♡ rebid.

12.

West	East
1♣(5++)	<u>1♡</u>(3+)
2NT	3NT

Note West needs ruffing value as well as 3 good hearts for raise in hearts.

13.

West	East
1♣(4++)	<u>1♡</u>(3–)
2♡	

14.

West	East
1♣(5)	<u>1♢</u>(2)
1♠	1NT
2♡	

Note West 'knows' that East has 4 not good hearts for this sequence.

15.	West	East
	1♣(4+)	1♡(3–)
	1NT	2◇

16.	West	East
	1♣(4+)	1◇(3–)
	1♠	Pass

17.	West	East
	1♣(5)	1◇(3–)
	1♠	1NT
	2♣	

18.	West	East
	1♣(5+)	1◇(3–)
	1♠	1NT
	2♡	

19.	West	East
	1♣(4+)	1♡(3–)
	1NT	2♣
	2◇	

20.	West	East
	1♣(5+)	1♡(3–)
	1NT	2♣

21.	West	East
	1♣(4+)	1◇(4)
	1♠	2♣
	2NT	3NT

22.	West	East
	1♣(4+)	1◇(4)
	1♠	2♣
	2♡	3NT

23.	West	East
	1♣(4+)	1◇(4)
	1♡	2♣
	2♡	2NT
	3NT	

Note how the choice of West's rebid steers the no trump contract in to the optimum hand (21, 22 and 23).

24.	West	East
	1♣(4++)	1♡(2)
	2♡	

West knows that East has 5+ suit since s/he cannot have a good 4.

Answers to Bidding Quiz 5 MIDMAC 1◇ Opening

1.	West	East
	1◇(6+)	1♠(3+)
	3♣	3NT

2.	West	East
	1◇(5+)	1♡(5)
	1♠(4++)	3NT

Without further ado East ensures the only contract is properly placed.

3.	West	East
	1◇(5)	2♠(4 p.t.)
	Pass(4+)	

4.	West	East
	1◇(5++)	1♠(4)
	1NT	2NT
	3NT	

5.	West	East
	1◇(5+)	1♠(3)
	1NT	2NT
	3NT	

6.	West	East
	1◇(4+)	1♡(3++)
	1♠(3+)	Pass

7. | West | East |
    |------|------|
    | 1◇(5) | 1♡(3+) |
    | 1NT | Pass |

8. | West | East |
    |------|------|
    | 1◇(5++) | 1♠(3) |
    | 1NT | Pass |

9. | West | East |
    |------|------|
    | 1◇(6++) | 1♡(3) |
    | 2♣(5+++) | 2◇ |
    | 4◇(6++) | 5◇(4) |

10. | West | East |
    |------|------|
    | 1◇(6+) | 1♡(3) |
    | 3◇ | 3NT |

11. | West | East |
    |------|------|
    | 1◇(5) | 1♠(4+) |
    | 2♣(4+) | 2♡ |
    | 2NT | 3NT |

Fourth suit forcing shows good 3+ suit and asks for partial stop, thus placing contract correctly.

12. | West | East |
    |------|------|
    | 1◇(6+) | 1♡(5+) |
    | 1♠(5++) | 4♠ |
    | 4NT(KCB) | 5♡ |
    | 6♠ | |

Answers to Bidding Quiz 6 MIDMAC 1◇ Opening

1. | West | East |
    |------|------|
    | 1◇(6–) | 1♠(3+) |
    | 2♡(5) | |

2. | West | East |
    |------|------|
    | 1◇(4+) | 2◇(4+) |
    | 2♠ | 3♡ |
    | 3NT | |

3. | West | East |
    |------|------|
    | 1◇(5++) | 2♣(8 p.t.) |
    | 3◇ | 4NT(KCB) |
    | 5♠ | 5NT |
    | 6◇ | 7♣ |

East knows immediately that the hand is worth 8 playing tricks because West promises 2+ clubs. Once West shows 5 diamonds and 4 key cards East can 'see' 13 tricks.

4. | West | East |
    |------|------|
    | 1◇(7+) | 2♣(4+) |
    | 4♠(9) | 4NT(6–)(KCB) |
    | 5♠ | 5NT |
    | 6♡ | 7♣ |

West is almost good enough for 1NT opener. Note CT is 15. East/West can in fact make 15 tricks!

5. | West | East |
    |------|------|
    | 1◇(5) | 3◇(5 p.t.) |
    | 3NT | |

West knows that combined controls are not enough for 5◇

6. | West | East |
    |------|------|
    | 1◇(5+) | 1NT(3) |
    | 2♡ | 3NT |

7. | West | East |
    |------|------|
    | 1◇(4++) | 2◇(4–) |
    | 2♠ | 3♣ |
    | 4♣(6) | Pass |

8. | West | East |
    |------|------|
    | 1◇(5) | 1♡(4) |
    | 1♠(4+) | 2♡ |
    | 2♠ | 3NT |

West's sequence shows exactly 3-0-5-5 because otherwise s/he would show longer minor by bidding it.

9.

West	East
1◇(5+)	**1♡(4+)**
1NT	2NT
3NT	

10.

West	East
1◇(4)	4♣(5-)

North/South won't find 4♡ or 4♠.

11.

West	East
1◇(5+++)	**1♠(4)**
1NT	2NT
3♡	4♡

If you don't get a heart lead you know where ♡K is!

12.

West	East
1◇(6)	**1♠(4+)**
2♣(5+)	2♡
3♡	4♡

2♡, fourth suit forcing, produces 3♡ confirming West is exactly 1-3-4-5 and maximum ... 5 tricks because otherwise s/he would have rebid 2NT. East can see 4♡ is a better contract than 3NT because of spade weakness, even on the standout trump lead.

Answers to Bidding Quiz 7 Part I.
Meaning of Opener's Rebids Following 1♠, 2♣

Rebid	Tricks	CV	Description
2◇	4	11-13	4+◇
2♡	4	11-13	4+♡
2♠	4	11-13	6+♠ (or good 5+ with 4 clubs)
2NT	4	11-13	balanced 5-3-3-2 type
3♣	5	14-16	4+♣
3◇	5/6	14-19	4+◇
3♡	5/6	14-19	4+♡
3♠	5/6	14-19	6+♠
3NT	5	14-16	balanced 5-3-3-2 type
4♣	6	17-19	4+good ♣
4◇	7	20-22	4◇ 4 good clubs ... void ♡
4♡	7	20-22	4♡ 4 good clubs ... void ◇
4♠	7(p.t.)	17-19	7+♠
4NT	6+	17-19	5-3-3-2 type some help in clubs
5♣	7	20-22	5 spades plus 5 clubs

Answers to Bidding Quiz 7 Part II
MIDMAC 1 Major Opening

1.

West	East
1♠(4+)	**2♦**(7)
2♠	**5♠**(7+)
6♠	

5♠ says to opener go to 6♠ if your trump quality is good.

2.

West	East
1♡(6+)	**2♣**(3+)
3♦	**3♠**
3NT	

East can see insufficient controls for a 5 level contract.

3.

West	East
1♡(5)	**1♠**(3)
2NT	3NT

4.

West	East
1♠(4)	**2♣**(4+)
2♦(4+)	**2♡**
3♣	4♠

A difficult hand to bid but note value of doubleton honours as support for five card major.

5.

West	East
1♡(4+)	**2♦**(4)
4♦(5+)	4♡

6.

West	East
1♠(5+)	**2♣**(4)
3♦	**3♡**(5−)
3♠	4♠

7.

West	East
1♡(6)	1NT(3+)
3♣	3♦
3♡	4♡(4)

or

West	East
1♡(6)	3♦(5 p.t.)
3♡	4♡

8.

West	East
1♠(5−)	1NT(3+)
2NT	3NT

9.

West	East
1♡(4)	2♠(4 p.t.)

Tough!

10.

West	East
1♠(6+)	Pass

What else?

11.

West	East
1♠(6)	**2♡**(4)
3♠	4♠

12.

West	East
1♠(8+p.t.)	**2♦**
3♠	4♠
4NT(KCB)	5♡
6♠(3++)	

Once East supports spades and has shown 3+ tricks it's only a question of how quick those tricks are, but it looks like it will depend on one of two finesses at worst.

Answers to Bidding Quiz 8 –
MIDMAC 2♣ & 2◇ Openers

1.

West	East
2♣(5+)	<u>2◇</u>(3)
2♡	<u>3♣</u>
3◇	4◇(4–)
5◇(5++)	

West naturally shows 0-3-4-6 shape with three good hearts and CV 14-16 East can see few wasted spade values and the only decision is whether to play in the 4-4◇ fit or the 6-2♣ fit!

2.

West	East
2♣(7 p.t.)	<u>2◇</u>(3)
3NT	

East can just squeak a response.

3.

West	East
2♣(5+)	3♡(5 p.t.)
4♡	

4.

West	East
2♣(6)	<u>2◇</u>(3+)
3◇	<u>3♡</u>
4♡	

West denies 3 good hearts but in raising to 4♡ shows good 2 or poor 3.

5.

West	East
2◇(4+)	2♡(8 p.t.)
2NT	<u>3♣</u>
3♡	<u>4NT</u>(KCB)
5♡	6♣

East knows West has at least 1 club!

6.

West	East
2◇(4)	<u>2♡</u>(6++)
2♠	3♣(7+)
4♣	6◇

East knows that West has 3-1-6-3 or conceivably 3-0-6-4, CV 11-13

7.

West	East
2♣(4)	2♡(4/5 p.t.)
Pass	

8.

West	East
2◇(5)	2♡(7)
3♣	<u>3♡</u>
3♠	6◇

West has described 3-0-6-4 or conceivably 3-1-6-3 with poor 3 card spade suit so East knows 6◇ is excellent depending on spade 'hook' at worst, if West has more values in clubs than diamonds.

9.

West	East
2♣(4+)	<u>2◇</u>(4+)
<u>2♠</u>	3NT

10.

West	East
2♣(7 p.t.)	<u>2◇</u>(5)
3♣	<u>3◇</u>
3♠	3NT

West shows good 2 or poor 3 spades so East can be first to bid 3NT to protect the heart suit.

11.

West	East
2◇(5+)	3♣(6 p.t.)
3♡	3NT

12.

West	East
2♣(5++)	<u>2◇</u>(6)
2♡	<u>2♠</u>
4♠(6++)	<u>4NT</u>(KCB)
5♠	7♠

West has naturally shown 3-3-1-6 with 3 aces.

Answers to Bidding Quiz 9 – MIDMAC 1NT Opener

1. West   East
1NT(8+)   __   2♣
2♢   3♠(2)
4NT(10+)(KCB) 5♢
6♠

2. West   East
1NT(7+)   3♡(5+p.t.)
4♡

West can see 5+ quick tricks to go with East's playing tricks.

3. West   East
1NT(7+)   2♣(2)
2NT   3♢
3♡   4♢
4♡

3♢ is transfer to 3♡.

4. West   East
1NT(9 p.t.s)2♣(1–)
3NT

5. West   East
1NT(8)   3♡(4 p.t.)
6NT

6. West   East
1NT(8+p.t.) 2♡(4)
3♣   3♢(4-)
3♠   3NT
4♣   6♣

4♣ is clearly setting the suit. East is a trick better than minimum.

7. West   East
1NT(9)   2♣(2)
2♢   2♡
4NT(10)(KCB) 5♢
6♡

8. West   East
1NT(9)   2♣(2)
2♢   3♣
3♡   4♡(3–)
4NT(KCB)   5♣
5♡

9. West   East
1NT(7+)   2♣(1+)
2NT   3NT

East denies 4+ major or good 5+ minor with 3NT rebid.

10. West   East
1NT(8+p.t.) 2♣(1)
3NT

11. West   East
1NT(9p.t.)   2♣(2–)
2♢   2♠
3♣   3♢
4♣   5♣

12. West   East
1NT(8p.t.)   2♣(2)
2♡   3♢
3NT

Answers to Bidding Quiz 10 –
More MIDMAC 1NT Openers

1.	West	East
	1NT(8+)	2NT(3+)
	3♣	3♡
	3♠	3NT
	4NT(Quant)	6NT

2.	West	East
	1NT(7++)	2♣(2–)
	2NT	3♡
	4♠(9+)	

West makes super accept when East shows at least five spades.

3.	West	East
	1NT(10+)	2♣(0)
	2◊	2NT
	3♠	3NT
	4◊	5◊(1)
	6◊	

4.	West	East
	1NT(7+)	2♣(2)
	2♠	2NT
	3◊	4♠(2+)

5.	West	East
	1NT(8+)	2♣(1)
	2◊	2NT
	3♣	3◊
	3♡	3♠
	4♠(9+)	

6.	West	East
	1NT(10p.t.)	2♡(4)
	3◊	4◊(4+)
	4NT(KCB)	5◊
	5NT	6◊
	7◊	

7.	West	East
	1NT(7)	2NT(3++)
	3♡	4NT(4+)(KCB)
	5♠	5NT
	6◊	6♡

8.	West	East
	1NT(7+)	2NT(3–)
	3♣	3♠
	5♠(9+)	6♠

9.	West	East
	1NT(7+)	2NT(3)
	3♣	3◊
	3♡	3NT
	4♣	5♣(3+)
	6♣(8+)	

10.	West	East
	1NT(7+)	2♣(2)
	2◊	2♠
	4♠(9)	

West uses the 2◊ bid to try and find a major fit telling a lie in the process. 4♠ is then less encouraging than 3♠.

11.	West	East
	1NT(7+)	3NT(5p.t.)
	6♣	

12.	West	East
	1NT(7++)	2♣(2+)
	2◊	3♡
	4NT(10)(KCB)	5◊
	7♡	

West knows that East has six poor hearts and the ♣A so can count 13 tricks. 'Wouldn't it be nice to finish with a flourish like that in the Bermuda Bowl Final?'

Answers to Bidding Quiz 11 MIDMAC Tops & Tips
(Hands From 1991 World Championship)

1.

West	East
1♣(6+++)	1◇(3)
2♠	3◇
3NT	4NT
5♠	6NT

4NT is quantitative Blackwood. The East hand is just too good for immediate 3◇ jump response. Only one out of eight pairs bid and made slam. The 6NT contract played by West is practically 70% which is good enough. Yes, the ♣A was onside but the ♠J did not fall in 3 rounds.

2.

West	East
1♡(5)	3♠(5/6p.t.)
Pass(4)	

All four pairs in the finals (Bermuda Bowl and Venice Cup) found game (2 in 4♠, 1 in 4♡ and 1 in 5◇) all going off. Did you have any problems finding a pass as opener after the 3♠ response on this misfit, particularly non-vulnerable?

3.

West	East
1◇(4)	2◇(6+)
2♡	2♠
3♣	3◇(8+)
3♡(i)	3♠(i)
4♣(i)	4NT(ii)
5◇	6◇

West shows exactly 2-3-3-5 without a spade stop (4 trick hand) plus ♡K ♣A and ◇Q which is all East needs to know to bid the odds on 6◇. The ♠K was onside and those North's who overcalled 1♠ made the slam even easier to visualise because it improved the odds positionally.

If North overcalls 1♠ the bidding goes:

1◇	(1♠)	Dble
2♣		2◇
3◇		3♡(i)
4♣(i)		4◇(i)
4♡(i)		6◇

4.

West	East
1♠(4+)	2♣(7/8p.t.)
2♠	3♣
3♡	3NT

5♣ goes off on a trump lead whilst 3NT is frigid for an overtrick. Most pairs were in 5♣. Note that if responder cannot force by simply rebidding clubs at the lowest level this hand is almost impossible to bid reliably to 3NT.

5.

West	East
1♣(6+)	1♠(5)
3♡	4♣
4◇(i)	4♠(i)
4NT(ii)	5♣
6♣	

West shows 6+ trick hand 1-4-4-4 and singleton spade honour, all East needs to have a shot at 6♣. Only 1 out of 4 bid 6♣ the others playing in 3NT.

Another hand where you would like to invite to slam depending on quality of the minor suit trump holding!

6.

West	East
1◇(6+)	1♠(7p.t.)
3♡	3♠
4♣	4NT(KCB)
5♠	7♠

West shows 6+ trick hand 1-3-4-5 with singleton spade honour and 3 aces so it is easy for East to bid 7♠.

7.	West	East
	1♣(6++)	1♦(3)
	2♥	3♦
	3♠	3NT

3NT is so much better than 5♣ but can only be reliably bid because West is able to undercut to confirm a great three card spade suit.

8.	West	East
	1♦(6)	2♦(5)
	4♠(8–)	6♦

West shows 7+ tricks with 3-1-5-4 or 3-0-5-5 shape including three spades to an honour.

9.	West	East
	1♣(4+)	1♦(4+)
	1♠	2♦
	2♠	3♣
	4♣	5♣(6)

Once West opens with this minimal hand it is easy to find 5♣ even if North/South intervene in the majors.

10.	West	East
	1♠(4+)	2NT(7)
	4♠(5)	5♣(i)
	5♦(i)	5♥(i)
	5♠	5NT(ii)
	6♥	7♠

West shows a 5 trick hand and extra spade length with the 4♠ rebid. Once West has cuebid diamonds and shown ♠A, East can see 7♠ is a great contract. Only one out of four found the grand in the finals.

11.	West	North	East
	1♠(5+++)	(2♣)	2NT(8–)
	3NT		4♣(i)
	4♦(i)		4♥(i)
	4NT(ii)		5♠
	6♠		

Only two of the four finalists found this absolutely frigid slam which made an overtrick at the table when the ♥J fell. The grand is actually fair since it makes on the ♣A lead or ♥J falling and on a diamond lead there are squeeze chances.

12.	West	North	East
	1♠(4+)	(2♥)	2NT(7-)
	3♣		3♥(i)
	4♣(i)		4♥(i)
	4NT(ii)		5♥
	6♠		

Once East responds 2NT, East/West can have a slow controlled auction. No pair found this superb slam, so take a bow if you did.

13.	West	North	East
	1♥(6+)	(2♠)	2NT(6–)
	4♦		4♠(i)
	5♣(i)		5♦(i)
	5NT(ii)		6♣
	6♥		

The last of a quartet of 2NT raises. Only two pairs found this worthwhile slam which always makes on careful play. ♥KQx were onside.

14.	West	East
	1♣(6++)	1♦(2)
	2♠	2NT
	3♣	3♠
	4♠	

Note that East hand is not suitable for initial 1NT response with such a poor heart suit holding. With ♠K offside and ◇A onside 5♣ and 3NT fail. 4♠ is the optimum and only making game which no pair found in either final.

15. West   East
       1♠(6++)   2◇(6--)
       3♠   4NT(KCB)
       5♣   6♠

Strange that no pair found this very reasonable and making 6♠ particularly since it was towards the end of the event when players are often starting to 'push'.

16. West   East
       1♡(4+)   1♠(5+)
       2♡   4♡(6)

2 out of 4 found this worthwhile vulnerable 22 HCP no-shortage game which is compensated for by having excellent combined controls of 9.

17. West   East
       1◇(4+)   1♡(5)
       1♠(3++)   2♡
       3◇   4♠

West shows 3-1-5-4 with three spades to an honour, just right for East to prefer the Moysian 4♠ to 4♡ or 3NT or 5◇ because East also knows that West's singleton H is not an honour. 4♠ will always make although no one bid it. 4♡ and 5◇ should always be one off with 3NT depending on the defence.

18. South   West   East
      1◇   Pass   3NT(8+ p.t.)

No pair found the frigid 3NT in the last gasp of the finals preferring 4♡ which is one off on the ◇AK lead and continuation. Note if South opens 1♣, East's hand is ideal for 3♣ which West is happy to convert to 3NT.

19. West   East
       2♣(5)   2♠(5/6 pt)
       4♠

Incredibly no Bermuda Bowl Quarter Finalist bid up to 4♠ usually defending 4♡. Note that the immediate 3♠ would show 6+ spades with at least 2 honours. 4♠ makes on '4D' declarer play.

20. West   East
       1◇(4++)   1♡(5)
       2♡   2♠(7-)(i)
       3♣(i)   3◇(i)
       3♡   4♣(i)
       4♠(i)   4NT(ii)
       5♡   6♡

Only half the field of eight pairs found this frigid 6♡

21. West   East
       1♡(6+)   1♠(3+)
       4♠(7+)

Three of the eight bid to the poor 6♠ despite the primary suit misfit.

22. In case you didn't pick it, this is a test for 4D thinking, third hand bidding and finding the only bid combined. The imaginative response by East of 3NT is designed to make life very uncomfortable for the opponents and it certainly does!

What would you do as South with:

♠ AK97x ♡ QJxx ◇AQx ♣ x

If you pass or double and lead a small spade East/West make their delightful 19 HCP game. What is for sure, North/South will not be able to find and make 4♡ or 4♠ now!

23.

West	East
1NT(7+)	**2♣**(2)
2♡	2♠(1)
2NT	3NT

Only one out of four pairs found the vastly superior 3NT and at that from the wrong side.

24.

West	East
1◊(5+)	**2◊**(5)
3NT	4◊
4♡(i)	4♠(i)
5♣(i)	6◊

Very few found this almost frigid 6◊ in the Round Robins.

• • • • •

Depending on your success or otherwise with those last world championship hands, you may be considering seriously taking up MIDMAC, or tiddlywinks.

Every new bidding system, or indeed, every proposed life-change is heralded by the energy, enthusiasm and ego of its advocate. I am the first to admit that it is all too easy to develop in isolation a theoretically ideal bidding system that is thwarted by partner's inability to properly understand and apply the principles. There is a fine balance between a simple, limited easy-to-assimilate system and a complex 'perfect' system beyond ordinary mortals. MIDMAC thrills me for many reasons, not the least of which is that it gets this balance right.

MIDMAC is unique for many reasons:

- Minimum and maximum critical suit length defined.
- Shape is shown naturally.
- Forcing situations absolutely clear cut.
- Responders jump new suit response never forcing.
- Slow or fast track for constructive or obstructive purpose.
- Facilitates optimum placement of no trump contracts.
- Suit pairs or teams equally.
- Unaffected by who happens to bid first.
- Aggressive opening bids.
- Forgiving of bidding slips.

… but I'm biased and persuade/protest too much.